The Hamlyn
Pressure
Cookbook
Jane Todd

HAMLYN
London . New York . Sydney . Toronto

Acknowledgements

The author and publisher would like to thank the following
for their help in supplying colour photographs for this book:
British Poultry Meat Association: page 57
Colman's Mustard: page 75
Danish Food Centre: pages 36 and 45
Gale's Honey: page 111
H. J. Heinz Company Limited: page 16
Knorr: page 18
M.E.A.T.: pages 46–7 and 48
Mushroom Growers Association: page 35
The Prestige Group Limited: pages 59 and 76
Taunton Cider: page 93
Tefal Housewares: page 94
Tower Housewares Limited: page 112

Photographs on pages 16, 18, 46–7, 48, 57, 59, 75, 76, 93, 94,
111 and 112 by John Lee

Illustrated by Gay John Galsworthy

Jacket photograph shows Pot-roast of pork with herbs
(see page 62)

Published by
The Hamlyn Publishing Group Limited
London . New York . Sydney . Toronto
Astronaut House, Feltham, Middlesex, England
© Copyright The Hamlyn Publishing Group Limited 1976

Seventh impression 1980

ISBN 0 600 37131 X

Printed in Hong Kong

Contents

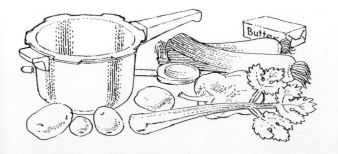

Useful Facts and Figures

Notes on metrication

In this book quantities have been given in Imperial and metric measures. Exact conversion from Imperial to metric measures does not usually give very convenient working quantities and so for greater convenience we have rounded off metric measures into units of 25 grammes. The table below shows recommended equivalents.

Ounces/ fluid ounces	Approx. g and ml to nearest whole figure	Recommended conversion to nearest unit of 25	Ounces/ fluid ounces	Approx. g and ml to nearest whole figure	Recommended conversion to nearest unit of 25
1	28	25	9	255	250
2	57	50	10 (½ pint)	283	275
3	85	75	15 (¾ pint)	425	425
4	113	100	16 (1 lb)	454	450
5 (¼ pint)	142	150	17	482	475
6	170	175	18	510	500
7	198	200	19	539	550
8 (½ lb)	226	225	20 (1 pint)	567	575

NOTE: When converting quantities over 20 oz, first add the appropriate figures in the centre column, then adjust to the nearest unit of 25. As a general guide, 1 kg (1000 g) equals 2.2 lb or about 2 lb 3 oz; 1 litre (1000 ml) equals 1.76 pints or almost exactly 1¾ pints.
Liquid measures The millilitre is a very small unit of measurement and we felt that to use decilitres (units of 100 ml) would be less cumbersome. In most cases it is perfectly satisfactory to round off the exact millilitre conversion to the nearest decilitre, except for ¼ pint; thus ¼ pint (142 ml) is 1.5 dl, ½ pint (283 ml) is 3 dl, ¾ pint (425 ml) is 4.5 dl, and 1 pint (567 ml) is 6 dl. For quantities over 1 pint we have used litres and fractions of a litre.
Can sizes Because at present cans are marked with the exact (usually to the nearest whole number) metric equivalent of the Imperial weight of the contents, we have followed this practice when giving can sizes.
Tablespoons Sometimes measurements are given in tablespoons; the spoon used is the British Standard measuring spoon of 17.7 millilitres.

All spoon measures are level unless indicated otherwise.

Measures for American users

DRY MEASURES

Imperial	American
1 lb butter	2 cups
1 lb flour	4 cups
1 lb dried fruit	3 cups
1 oz flour	¼ cup
1 oz sugar	2 tablespoons
1 oz butter	2 tablespoons

LIQUID MEASURES

¼ pint liquid	⅔ cup
(e.g. milk, stock, water etc.)	
½ pint liquid	1¼ cups
1 pint liquid	2½ cups
2 pints liquid	5 cups

NOTE: The British pint measures 20 fluid ounces whereas the American pint equals 16 fluid ounces.

Introduction

Although the principle of cooking foods by steam pressure has been known since 1679 when Denis Papin, a French physicist, invented 'The Papin Digester' a saucepan with an airtight lid which incorporated a safety valve, it was not until 1947 when pressure cookers started to come into the shops. Since then, as with all appliances, many changes in design have taken place and the pressure cooker is now regarded by many as an essential piece of kitchen equipment.

There are certainly many advantages to cooking foods under pressure, particularly in these days of rising fuel costs when everyone is attempting to cut fuel bills. By using a pressure cooker, foods are cooked in a quarter of the cooking time taken by other methods which must represent, even over a relatively short period, a reduced gas or electricity bill. Stewing beef, boiling fowls and less young game birds all benefit from being pressure cooked; working mums and bachelor cooks will find owning a pressure cooker a great asset when a meal has to be prepared and served in a short time, and when cooking facilities are limited. Today, many people have discovered the freedom of a self-catering holiday in a caravan, a boat or under canvas and have found a pressure cooker invaluable as it can do the work of one or two ordinary pans.

I hope that by reading this book and using the recipes you will learn to regard your pressure cooker as one of the greatest assets in your kitchen. You won't find any cake recipes in the book as I have only given ones which ideally lend themselves to pressure cooking. When you have tried some of my recipes I hope you will be inspired to develop your own and widen the range of your menus for family and friends.

I would like to extend my thanks to Dianne Page of Tower Housewares, and to The Prestige Group and Tefal Housewares for their help and advice.

Jane Todd

Glossary

A list of special terms used in a book is always helpful. The terms which apply to the pressure cooker are also explained, in greater detail, in the chapter beginning on page 8.

Beurre manié A mixture of equal quantities of butter and plain flour kneaded together. Small pieces of the mixture are whisked into a soup, sauce or casserole, over a moderate heat, to thicken it, at the end of cooking.

Blanch To place food in boiling water to remove skins, a bitter taste, or to whiten. Also used to partly cook vegetables prior to freezing.

Blend A term used to describe the process of blending soups, sauces, fruit, etc. in a liquidiser, to make a smooth mixture.

Bouquet garni A selection of fresh herbs (usually parsley, thyme, peppercorns and a bay leaf) tied together in a piece of muslin and added to soups and stews. Also available in sachets. Remove before serving.

Breadcrumbs Fresh crumbs made from day-old white bread used for coating foods for frying, or for stuffing and meat loaves.

Croûtons Small even-sized cubes of bread fried in oil (or oil and butter) and used as a garnish for soups and savoury dishes. Croûtons may be frozen.

Gasket The sealing ring between the lid and the base of the pressure cooker.

Infuse To steep foods in a hot liquid to extract flavour.

Marinade A liquid usually made with cider, wine, vinegar, oil and herbs. Used for soaking meat and fish prior to cooking. The marinade may also be used in the cooking.

Pressure weight The part of the cooker used to indicate the pressures. Not to be immersed in water.

Purée A mixture pressed through a sieve to remove pips, etc., or blended in the liquidiser.

Reduce To boil a liquid over a high heat (uncovered) to evaporate some of the water content in order to make the liquid more concentrated.

Rotating valve An alternative to the pressure weight.

Sauté Meat, poultry and vegetables may be lightly fried before the main cooking to give a good flavour and colour to the finished dish.

Separator Part of the pressure cooker used for cooking different foods at the same time, and to prevent cross flavours.

Stock A liquid used in soups and casseroles; for cooking meat, poultry and fish. Beef, chicken or fish stock may be used. Stock may also be prepared from beef, chicken or mixed herb cubes.

Trivet Part of the pressure cooker used to stand foods (or the separators) on. May also be used as a divider.

Truss A term applied to poultry and game where the bird is tied into a neat shape for cooking.

All about Pressure Cookers

Today there is a wide range of pressure cookers to choose from, but the basic principle on which they all operate is the same–when you place your cooker on the gas or electric ring or the hot plate of a solid fuel cooker and apply heat to the base of the cooker, the liquid inside begins to boil. When cooking in an ordinary saucepan the steam produced escapes into the surrounding air. A pressure cooker is so designed to seal in and control the steam which normally escapes. When the steam is trapped the pressure and temperature inside the cooker rise allowing the food in the cooker to cook much more quickly than it would in a casserole dish in the oven, or in a saucepan on top of the cooker. Cooking food under pressure can result in cutting certain cooking times by as much as 75%.

Most cookers are made from stainless steel or aluminium and, to fit in with the colour scheme of your kitchen and other appliances, they are available in a high gloss coloured finish, or the exterior may be polished. The handles are made of a heat-resistant material; a pressure cooker also comes with a pressure weight, trivet and separators. Some pressure cookers have only one pressure–there is a model which operates at $7\frac{1}{2}$ lb pressure and one which operates at 15 lb pressure.

Your choice of cooker will naturally be a matter of personal preference and needs. When choosing a cooker it is worth noting the following points:
1 Buy a cooker which will be adequate for the amount and type of cooking you intend to do. The smallest model available will not be of much use to you if at every meal time you have to cater for a large family. The price difference between the smallest and largest models is in the region of £6. Also, decide whether you want a cooker which operates at different pressures, or a

model which has the one pressure. (The bottling process for vegetables must be carried out under 10 lb
pressure.) For general recipes a one-pressure model is
adequate, but with the $7\frac{1}{2}$ lb pressure model some of the
cooking times will obviously be longer than those given
in this book.
2 At the time of purchase, check that replacement
parts are available, should you, for example, throw the
essential weight away with the potato peelings! Also
make sure that the manufacturer offers a guarantee.
3 If you are hooked on non-stick pans, choose a pressure
cooker with a non-stick interior.
4 In order to get the best from your cooker read the
manufacturer's instruction leaflet carefully and adhere
to it especially with regard to assembling and using the
cooker. Should you have any queries regarding your
cooker, do write to the manufacturer who will be only
too willing to help.

Having purchased your cooker make sure that you use
it to advantage. It is very easy to keep your shiny new
piece of labour- and time-saving equipment tucked
away in its box at the back of a remote kitchen cupboard.
I keep mine along with my other saucepans; having said
that I must add that it is equally important to make
sure that your pressure cooker doesn't become knocked
about in the *mêlée* of your other pots and pans! If the
rims of the lid or body are damaged, steam and therefore
pressure could be lost.

Advantages of using a pressure cooker

Foods cooked under pressure obviously cook more
quickly resulting in, over the long term, a tremendous
fuel saving. With the ever-increasing costs of all types
of fuel I think it makes sense to use a pressure cooker.

Further economies can be achieved as more than
one type of food—even complete meals—may be cooked
simultaneously.

A pressure cooker can be used in conjunction with
other kitchen equipment. For example, when freezing
down vegetables a pressure cooker may be used for the
blanching process—accurate timing is essential. It also
comes into its own when you are having a cook-up of
soups, casseroles, etc., for the freezer. When preparing
soups you may also want to use your liquidiser.

With all types of cooking there is inevitably some loss of nutritive value but with the comparatively short pressure cooking time, small amount of liquid used and the absence of light and air, this nutritive loss is certainly cut down to a minimum.

The so-called cheaper cuts of meat, shin for example, which is full of flavour, become beautifully tender when cooked under pressure.

A pressure cooker is equally suitable for the family and for bachelor cooks.

A pressure cooker is a splendid piece of equipment to take on a self-catering holiday whether you plan to rent a flat by the sea, a motor cruiser or pitch your own tent.

Some foods do have a somewhat unpleasant aroma—the smell of cabbage for example when being cooked in an ordinary saucepan, tends to permeate the whole house so that the family know in advance what is on the menu and can be put off before the food even appears on the table. Both the steam and cooking smells are sealed in the pressure cooker until the end of the cooking time. Less steam means less condensation.

Dried vegetables (split peas, lentils, etc.) don't need overnight soaking.

How to use your pressure cooker

The parts explained
It is most important that you follow the manufacturer's instructions which apply to your particular type of

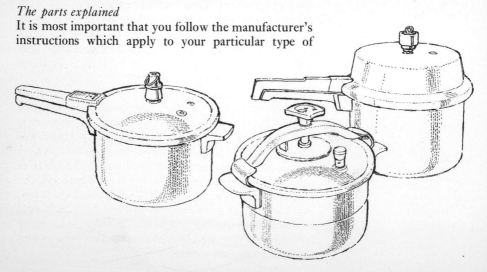

cooker. All pressure cookers have a pressure weight or a rotating valve (this applies to the cookers which operate at $7\frac{1}{2}$ lb pressure only), but the design may vary according to the type of cooker.

The pressure weight

This enables three different pressures to be used– 5, 10 and 15 lb. Throughout this book I have referred to the cooking pressures as either low, medium or high. As a general guide, the *low* pressure is used for steamed sweet and savoury puddings, fruit bottling, *medium* pressure is for jams, jellies and chutneys, and *high pressure* for marmalade making, cereal-type puddings, fruit puddings, meat and poultry dishes, vegetables, fish, soups and stock.

There are two main types of weight. *Type A*, shown in the drawing, has a central plunger marked with three silver rings. As the pressure rises and falls in the cooker, the plunger also rises and falls. When the first ring is visible this indicates that *low* pressure has been reached; when two rings are visible, *medium* pressure has been reached; when all three rings are visible, *high* pressure has been reached.

With *Type B* weight, the pressure is changed by adding or taking off one or two pieces of the weight. Simply unscrew the successive rings. To cook under *high* pressure all three must be used; remove the outer one when *medium* pressure is required and use only the central weight for *low* pressure. When putting a weight on the cooker, simply press down and the weight will click into position. It must not be screwed on.

Before opening a pressure cooker, the weight must be removed, but remember not to remove the weight until the pressure has been fully reduced (see page 16).

The trivet

This part of a pressure cooker is used when you want the food to cook in steam as opposed to liquid. For example, you don't use the trivet when cooking soups and casseroles, but you do use it when cooking a pot roast. The liquid (*always* necessary in a pressure cooker) is poured into the bottom of the cooker, the trivet is then put in position with the rim downwards and the food put on top of the trivet. The food cooks in the steam, produced under pressure, and no cross flavours occur. The trivet can also be used to divide different foods, or as a platform for one ovenproof container to be placed securely on top of another.

Type A *pressure weight showing the central plunger with the three rings visible to indicate that high pressure has been reached.*

Type B *pressure weight. With this type the pressure is changed by adding or taking off one or two pieces of the weight.*

The trivet

With the larger models of some pressure cookers, a set of three legs is provided to make a greater area below the trivet to accommodate more food.

To remove the trivet, with or without the food on it, simply hook a fork into one of the slots and lift.

The separators
These are for cooking different foods at the same time, and prevent cross flavours. They also make it easier to remove the food from the pressure cooker. Depending on your model, you may have either two or three separators. They can be perforated or solid–the perforated ones are for cooking vegetables and the solid ones are used for cooking rice, stewed fruit, milk puddings, etc. I also find the solid separators ideal for reheating a frozen portion of casserole, etc.

The separators are placed on the trivet in the bottom of the cooker (remembering to put the minimum amount of liquid in the bottom of the cooker), or on the trivet which may be placed on top of a casserole in the bottom of the cooker.

The separators

The sealing gasket
This seals the gap between the lid and base to make the pressure cooker airtight.

Safety devices
All pressure cookers incorporate safety devices which come into operation automatically when needed. They will operate if:
1 The centre vent pipe should become blocked.
2 The pressure cooker should boil dry. At this point I must add that if you fully understand the workings of your pressure cooker and have read the manufacturer's leaflet carefully, the safety device need never come into action. I have a friend who remembers her mother's efforts at pressure cooking and believes that her food is going to be firmly splattered all over the ceiling. I can assure you that this won't happen if you stick to the simple and basic rules of pressure cooking. I think more and more of us, through necessity, are becoming freezer-minded and have adjusted our shopping and cooking habits to suit. In the same way, one needs to adjust slightly to become pressure cooker-minded.

Step-by-step guide to pressure cooking
In the recipes in this book, I have always given concise details in the method according to the type of recipe. In

a *Place the trivet in the base of the pressure cooker.*

the step-by-step drawings here you can see the basic method to follow when cooking a different vegetable in the two separators. Whatever type of food you are cooking these basic rules always apply. Again, I must stress the importance of referring to the manufacturer's leaflet which will be applicable to your particular pressure cooker.

1 Place the trivet in the base of the cooker. Pour in the accurately measured amount of liquid for the recipe being followed. The liquid used in pressure cooking must be one which gives off steam when it reaches boiling point—water, stock, wine or milk. The amount of liquid required depends on the length of cooking, *not* on the amount of food being cooked. With most models, the minimum of liquid needed is $\frac{1}{2}$ pint (3 dl). With some smaller models and if the cooking time is under 15 minutes, $\frac{1}{4}$ pint (1.5 dl) liquid is the minimum requirement.

2 Place the prepared vegetables in the separators and season lightly. Always ensure that sufficient space is left above the food for the steam to circulate. A pressure cooker must not be filled more than two-thirds full of solid food—joints of meat, chops, vegetables, etc. Less solid foods and ones which tend to boil over, such as

b *Pour in the measured amount of liquid. The liquid used in a pressure cooker must be one which gives off steam when it reaches boiling point.*

c *Sprinkle the prepared vegetables (placed in the separators) with a little salt.*

soups, casseroles, pasta, milk puddings, etc., must only half fill the cooker as they need space to rise as they come to the boil.

Foods which you are cooking simultaneously must all have the same cooking time, or root vegetables must be cut small so that they cook in the same time as, for example, sprouts.

3 Place the cooker on the source of heat, but do not turn the heat on yet. Fit the lid on the cooker and align the handle of the lid with that of the body of the cooker. It is most important to fit the lid on properly before applying the heat which will start to bring the liquid to the boil.

4 If your cooker has a *Type A* pressure weight, place it firmly on the vent pipe so that it clicks into position. Turn the heat to high and wait for the steam to come out of the air vent in the lid of the cooker.

If your cooker has a *Type B* pressure weight, turn the heat on to high (without the weight in position) and wait until a steady flow of steam comes from the centre vent—don't go away from the cooker during this short period—then place the correct weight (low, medium or high) on the centre vent, pushing it down until a slight click is heard.

f *With Type B pressure weight, turn the heat on to high and when a steady flow of steam appears, place the weight in position.*

d *Fix the lid in position and place on the source of heat.*

e *With Type A pressure weight, place it firmly on the vent pipe so that it clicks into position.*

5 With *Type A* pressure weight, wait for the air vent to rise and seal the cooker, then watch the plunger rise from the weight until the required pressure is reached—this is indicated by the number of silver rings showing (see page 11). When the required pressure is reached, reduce the heat to low to maintain that pressure and calculate the cooking time from then. If the pressure drops (i.e. the plunger drops) increase the heat slightly.

With *Type B* pressure weight, a slight hissing sound will be heard followed by a louder one. This indicates that the cooker has reached the pressure according to the weight selected. Lower the heat to obtain a steady, gentle sound and calculate the cooking time from then, maintaining the same sound throughout the cooking period.

6 At the end of the calculated cooking time, turn off the heat. If you are cooking on an electric ring or solid fuel hot plate, gently draw the cooker away from the source of heat as with these types of cooker a certain amount of residual heat will remain and could cause the food inside the pressure cooker to become overcooked.

The pressure now has to be reduced and can be done in two ways—*never attempt to remove the weight or open the cooker until the pressure has been fully reduced.*

g *With Type A pressure weight, wait until the required pressure has been reached (indicated by number of rings visible), then lower the heat to maintain that pressure for the calculated cooking time.*

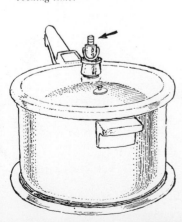

h *At the end of the cooking time, carefully remove the cooker from the heat (with a gas burner simply turn off the heat).*

To reduce the pressure at room temperature This is referred to as reducing the pressure slowly. Leave the cooker to stand at room temperature, away from the heat.

To reduce the pressure quickly Either stand the cooker in a bowl of cold water, or run cold water from the top over the outsides of the cooker being careful not to allow it to run into the centre vent, or the air vent. 7 Before removing the lid from the cooker, ensure that the pressure has reduced completely. With *Type A* check that the indicator weight plunger has returned to the normal position, i.e. with no silver rings visible, and that the air vent has returned to normal position. Remove the indicator weight with a fork and only then remove the lid.

With *Type B* lift the tip of the weight slightly and if there is no escape of steam the weight may be removed and then the lid.

Note
With pressure cooking timing is crucial. I find it helpful to set a 'pinger' to remind me when the cooking time is completed.

j Before removing the lid check that the pressure has reduced completely. With Type A weight the rings will not be visible and the weight may be removed by lifting it with the prongs of a fork

i To reduce the pressure quickly, place the cooker in a bowl of cold water.

With Type B weight lift the tip of the weight slightly. If there is an escape of steam, the pressure has not completely reduced.

16

Beef and bean savoury (see page 96)

When cooking foods such as soups, casseroles, egg custards, milk puddings, suet puddings and when bottling, the pressure should always be reduced at room temperature. If the pressure was reduced quickly (by the cold water method) semi-liquid foods could froth up and spurt out of the air vent, egg custards could curdle, suet puddings could sink and jars (for bottling) could crack, all due to the too sudden drop in temperature. With vegetables the pressure should be reduced quickly to avoid the vegetables becoming overcooked.

How to use a pressure cooker which operates at one pressure ($7\frac{1}{2}$ lb)

1 *To put on the lid* Slide the lid on horizontally and fit it onto the rim of the cooker. Ensure that the lid is centred and that it fits correctly onto the base of the cooker. Turn the knob on the lid in the direction of the arrow to fix the clamp in position.

2 *To tighten the lid* Turn the knob through two complete turns–the lid is then properly locked.

3 *To insert the rotating valve* Place the valve vertically in position on the flange on the lid and push down as far as it will go.

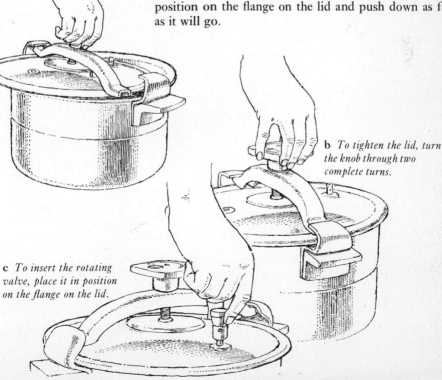

a *To put on the lid, slide it on horizontally under the lugs.*

b *To tighten the lid, turn the knob through two complete turns.*

c *To insert the rotating valve, place it in position on the flange on the lid.*

Watercress and potato soup (see page 28), celery soup (see page 25) and French onion soup (see page 27)

4 *Place the cooker on the heat* When the rotating valve begins to turn (steam will escape from the valve) pressure has been reached and the cooking time is calculated from then. Reduce the heat so that the valve remains still (a small amount of steam will escape from time to time) and cook for the calculated time according to your recipe.

The recipes in this book may be used with a cooker which operates at $7\frac{1}{2}$ lb pressure, but you will need to increase the cooking times where a medium or high pressure is indicated in the recipes. As a guide, where high pressure is indicated, allow double the cooking time, also remembering to double the amount of liquid in the recipe.

5 *To reduce the pressure* Remove the cooker from the heat. Lift the rotating valve up to the first notch to allow the steam to escape and lower the pressure inside the cooker. When all the steam has been released, remove the lid.

6 *To remove the lid* Turn the knob in the opposite direction of the arrow, through two complete turns. Lift the lid and slide it out horizontally.

Note

Do not allow this type of pressure cooker to cool without reducing the pressure, otherwise a vacuum will form and it will be impossible to remove the lid. Should this happen, apply heat to the base and this will enable the lid to be slid off horizontally.

f *At the end of the cooking time, turn off the heat and reduce the pressure. When the pressure has reduced, remove the lid by turning the knob in the opposite direction of the arrow, through two complete turns.*

e *When the rotating valve turns, lower the heat so that the valve remains still and calculate the cooking from then.*

d *Place the cooker on the heat.*

Care of your pressure cooker

As with any new appliance, it is essential to treat your pressure cooker with care so that it will reward you with many years of service.

Wash the cooker in warm soapy water and dry. Do not use washing soda as this will cause discoloration. If you live in a hard water area the inside of your cooker may discolour; this discoloration can be removed by using soap-filled pads (not to be used on non-stick linings), or by boiling up some apple peelings and water in the cooker.

After every use check that the vent pipe and air vent are clear. If blocked, clean under hot running water with the aid of a skewer.

Although the handles are made of a heat-resistant material, avoid leaving them over direct heat, particularly when reducing the pressure at room temperature.

The sealing gasket needs to be removed and cleaned frequently. Wait until the gasket has cooled before putting it back in place.

Store your pressure cooker with the lid upside down to allow the free circulation of air and help prevent odours. However, if you own a pressure cooker which operates at $7\frac{1}{2}$ lb pressure do not invert the lid when the cooker is not in use as the clamp may become fixed under the lugs.

Take care not to dent the lid or base as if either of these parts do not align and completely seal the cooker it will not work efficiently.

If your model has a non-stick lining, give it the respect it deserves. Avoid using metal utensils and harsh scouring pads. Before using a non-stick pressure cooker for the first time, wash the coated surface in hot, soapy water and dry with a soft cloth.

Manufacturers do offer a repairing and re-conditioning service. Any necessary replacement parts will also be available direct from the manufacturer.

Store your pressure cooker with the lid upside down to allow the free circulation of air.
Note: *Do not store the type which operates at $7\frac{1}{2}$ lb pressure this way as the clamp may become fixed under the lugs.*

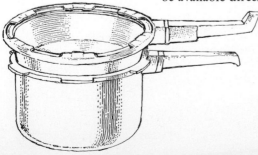

Ten golden rules to pressure cooking

The liquid used must be one which gives off steam when it boils. Fat or oil is not suitable.

The total amount of liquid used must be put in the cooker before it is brought to pressure.

The quantity of liquid is calculated according to the total pressure cooking time, *not* the amount of food being cooked.

Meat and poultry may be sealed in fat or oil before pressure cooking, in which case you use the cooker as an ordinary pan for this process.

Always allow sufficient space above the food for the steam to circulate. Do not fill the cooker more than two-thirds full with solid foods and not more than half full with liquid and semi-liquid foods.

The lid must be correctly sealed before bringing the cooker up to pressure.

Calculate the cooking time from the moment the cooker has come to the required pressure for each particular recipe.

When the cooking time is up, allow the pressure to reduce before opening the cooker.

Foods can only be cooked simultaneously if they all require the same pressure and cooking times. To pressure cook vegetables (for example, new potatoes) to serve as an accompaniment to a beef casserole, reduce the pressure 4–5 minutes before the end of the calculated cooking time, add the prepared and *lightly* salted vegetables placed in the separator, bring back to pressure and cook for 4–5 minutes.

If in doubt about any point, refer to the manufacturer's leaflet. It has been compiled to help you— don't throw it away with the packing!

Soups

Home-made soups are ideal for both families and entertaining. They also make a welcome midday snack with hot crusty French bread, croûtons, garlic bread or toast at the weekend.

The basis of a soup is a good stock which I admit can be made with those very convenient cubes, available in beef, chicken or mixed herb flavours, but with the aid of a pressure cooker it can be cooked in 40 minutes. Stock may be frozen in polythene containers or ice cube trays for future use.

I am very fond of soups made with the pulses—split peas and lentils—and these do take a long time to cook in an ordinary pan. Pressure-cooked lentil soup takes 10 minutes at high pressure.

Most soups are good freezer candidates, so it is always a great saving to make more than you require immediately and freeze the remainder for future use. The great drawback I find with soups from the freezer is that they take an incredibly long time to thaw over a gentle heat. I now put mine in the solid separators, placed on the trivet (remembering to put $\frac{1}{2}$ pint (3 dl) water in the bottom of the pressure cooker) and pressure cook for 8 minutes at high pressure. What a bonus! So that the frozen block of soup can be accommodated in the separator, line the separator with a small polythene bag. Three-quarters fill with the cooled soup and open freeze until solid. You can remove the separator and wrap, seal and label your stock or soup which is the perfect shape and fit for reheating in the separator, under pressure. Do remember to remove the polythene bag before putting the soup into the separator.

Rules for pressure cooking soups

1 The trivet is not used in soup making.

2 High pressure is used. When making a soup with dried vegetables (split peas, lentils, etc.) bring to high pressure on a low heat to prevent frothing up.

3 If the vegetables are sautéed, this is done in the open cooker. The thickening and enriching agents are added after the main cooking. If a soup is liquidised after cooking it does not usually require any further thickening. A swirl of cream may be added to enhance the eye appeal of the soup.

4 When you have added all the ingredients to the pan check that it is not more than half full. If you are doubling up the quantities it may be necessary to cook the soup in two batches which still uses less fuel than cooking in an ordinary pan.

5 Do not be too heavy handed with seasoning and flavouring ingredients. Usually less is needed as the vegetables retain more of their own natural mineral salts.

6 Allow the pressure to reduce at room temperature.

Stock

COOKING TIME 40 minutes
PRESSURE high
MAKES 2 pints (generous
 1 litre)

2 lb/1 kg meat bones
2 pints/generous 1 litre
 water
2 onions, quartered
1–2 carrots, quartered
2–3 sticks celery, halved
few peppercorns
1 bay leaf
¼ teaspoon salt
few sprigs parsley

Wash the bones and break up as small as possible. Place the bones and water in the open cooker (with the trivet removed) and bring slowly to the boil. With a slotted draining spoon, remove the scum that rises to the top. Add the remaining ingredients, making sure that the cooker is not more than half full. Bring to high pressure and cook for 40 minutes. Allow the pressure to reduce at room temperature. Strain, allow to cool, then remove the fat from the surface. Keep the stock in the refrigerator for up to 4 days.

To make *chicken stock*, use a chicken carcase in place of the meat bones.

To freeze

When cold, freeze in polythene tumblers, leaving a small headspace, or if more convenient, in ice cube trays. Cubes of beef or chicken stock are handy when a few tablespoonfuls are required.

Celery Soup

COOKING TIME 10 minutes
PRESSURE high
SERVES 4

1 oz/25 g butter
1 head celery, prepared
 and chopped
1½ pints/9 dl stock, made
 with 2 chicken stock cubes
1 blade mace
1 bay leaf
salt and pepper
squeeze lemon juice
¼ pint/1.5 dl single cream
Thickening (optional)
1 oz/25 g flour
1 oz/25 g butter
Garnish
few celery leaves
paprika
Illustrated on page 18

Heat the butter in the cooker (with the trivet removed) and sauté the chopped celery for 5 minutes. Add the stock, herbs, seasoning and lemon juice making sure that the cooker is not more than half full. Bring to high pressure and cook for 10 minutes.

Allow the pressure to reduce at room temperature. Either press the soup through a sieve or blend in a liquidiser, remembering to discard the herbs. Return to the open cooker and reheat. (If the soup has been sieved, thicken it by whisking in small pieces of the butter and flour blended together.) Check the seasoning and just before serving stir in the cream. Garnish with a few celery leaves and a sprinkling of paprika.

To freeze

When cold, freeze in polythene containers, leaving a small headspace, or foil bags. Stir in the cream at the reheating stage.

Cream of Artichoke Soup

Wash and peel the artichokes, cut into thin slices. Heat the butter in the open cooker (with the trivet removed) and sauté the artichokes and onion for 5 minutes without allowing them to brown. Add the seasoning, stock, bouquet garni and lemon juice, making sure that the cooker is not more than half full. Bring to high pressure and cook for 10 minutes.

Allow the pressure to reduce at room temperature. Remove the bouquet garni, then liquidise the soup. Check the seasoning, mix the egg yolks and cream together then stir into the soup. Reheat, but do not boil. Just before serving stir in the chopped parsley.

To freeze

When cold, freeze in polythene containers, leaving a small headspace, or foil bags. Stir in the egg yolks and cream at the reheating stage.

COOKING TIME 10 minutes
PRESSURE high
SERVES 4

1 lb/0.5 kg Jerusalem
  artichokes
1 oz/25 g butter
1 onion, chopped
salt and pepper
2 pints/generous 1 litre
  chicken stock or water
bouquet garni
1 teaspoon lemon juice
2 egg yolks
4 tablespoons cream
1–2 tablespoons chopped
  parsley

Celery and Mushroom Soup

Place the prepared vegetables in the cooker (with the trivet removed) and add the tomato juice, stock, seasoning, Worcestershire sauce and bouquet garni, making sure that the cooker is not more than half full. Bring to high pressure and cook for 10 minutes.

Allow the pressure to reduce at room temperature. Discard the bouquet garni and check the seasoning. The soup may be served as it is, pressed through a sieve or blended in the liquidiser. Serve garnished with a few raw mushroom slices.

COOKING TIME 10 minutes
PRESSURE high
SERVES 4–6

8 oz/225 g carrots, sliced
12 oz/350 g onions, chopped
1 head celery, sliced
8 oz/225 g mushrooms,
  sliced
4 oz/100 g French or runner
  beans, sliced
1 pint/6 dl tomato juice
1 pint/6 dl beef stock
salt and pepper
$\frac{1}{2}$–1 tablespoon
  Worcestershire sauce
bouquet garni
Garnish
few mushroom slices
Illustrated on page 35

26

Cream of Mushroom Soup

COOKING TIME 5 minutes
PRESSURE high
SERVES 4–6

1 lb/0.5 kg mushrooms
2 oz/50 g butter
1 small clove garlic,
  crushed
1½ pints/9 dl chicken stock
salt and pepper
pinch nutmeg
¼ pint/1.5 dl cream
2 tablespoons chopped
  parsley
Thickening
1 oz/25 g butter
1 oz/25 g flour

Wash and dry the mushrooms, and slice thinly–the stalks may be used as well. Heat the butter in the open cooker (with the trivet removed) and sauté the mushrooms and garlic for 5 minutes. Add the chicken stock, salt and pepper and nutmeg, making sure that the cooker is not more than half full. Bring to high pressure and cook for 5 minutes.

Allow the pressure to reduce at room temperature. Thicken the soup by whisking in small pieces of the butter and flour blended together. Check the seasoning and just before serving stir in the cream and chopped parsley.

To freeze

When cold, freeze in polythene containers, leaving a small headspace, or foil bags. Stir in the cream and parsley at the reheating stage.

French Onion Soup

COOKING TIME 4 minutes
PRESSURE high
SERVES 4

1 lb/0.5 kg onions
2 oz/50 g butter
2 pints/generous 1 litre
  stock, made with 2 beef
  stock cubes
salt and pepper
1 bay leaf
few drops Worcestershire
  sauce or 1 tablespoon
  Madeira per serving
4 slices French bread
4 oz/100 g Gruyère or
  Cheddar cheese, grated
Garnish
chopped parsley
Illustrated on page 18

Peel and thinly slice the onions. Heat the butter in the open cooker (with the trivet removed) and sauté the onions over a very low heat for 10 minutes, until the onions are softened and just beginning to brown. To obtain a good, rich flavour to this soup it is important to cook the onions slowly at this stage. Add the stock, seasoning and bay leaf, making sure that the cooker is not more than half full. Bring to high pressure and cook for 4 minutes.

Allow the pressure to reduce at room temperature. Remove the bay leaf, then ladle the soup into four ovenproof bowls. Stir either a few drops of Worcestershire sauce or 1 tablespoon Madeira into each bowl of soup, then add a slice of French bread. Sprinkle the bread with a generous amount of grated cheese, then put the bowls of soup under a preheated grill for 2–3 minutes, until the cheese is bubbling. Serve garnished with chopped parsley.

To freeze

Freeze the soup without the bread and cheese.

Minestrone

The vegetables used in a minestrone soup may be varied according to what is available, but there must always be a good selection. Any shape of pasta may be used–spirals, twists, spaghetti–broken into short lengths –and if liked dried beans may also be added.

Rind and chop the bacon rashers. Chop the carrots, onion and celery; finely shred the cabbage and peel and chop the tomatoes.

Place the bacon in the open cooker (with the trivet removed) and sauté over a moderate heat until the fat begins to run. Add the oil and the prepared carrots, onion, celery and cabbage. Sauté over a low heat for 5 minutes. Add the garlic, tomatoes, macaroni, stock, bay leaf and seasoning, making sure that the cooker is not more than half full. Bring to high pressure and cook for 8 minutes.

Allow the pressure to reduce at room temperature. Remove the bay leaf, stir in the tomato purée and check the seasoning. Serve sprinkled with grated Parmesan cheese.

COOKING TIME 8 minutes
PRESSURE high
SERVES 6

2–3 rashers streaky bacon
2 carrots
1 onion
4 sticks celery
8 oz/225 g cabbage
2 tomatoes
1 tablespoon oil
1 clove garlic, crushed
2–3 oz/50–75 g short-cut macaroni
2 pints/generous 1 litre chicken stock or water
1 bay leaf
salt and pepper
1 tablespoon tomato purée
grated Parmesan cheese

Watercress and Potato Soup

This soup really needs to be blended in the liquidiser.

Peel and cube the potatoes, chop the onion and wash the watercress–both the stalks and leaves are used. Heat the butter in the open cooker (with the trivet removed) and sauté the chopped onion for 3–4 minutes, without allowing it to brown. Add the potatoes, watercress, seasoning, nutmeg and stock, making sure that the cooker is not more than half full. Bring to high pressure and cook for 10 minutes.

Allow the pressure to reduce at room temperature. Blend the slightly cooled soup in the liquidiser until smooth. Return to the open cooker, check the seasoning, reheat and stir in the cream just before serving. Serve garnished with a few watercress leaves.

To freeze

When cold, freeze in polythene containers, leaving a small headspace, or foil bags. Stir in the cream at the reheating stage.

COOKING TIME 10 minutes
PRESSURE high
SERVES 4–6

8 oz/225 g potatoes
1 onion
1 bunch watercress
1 oz/25 g butter
salt and pepper
pinch nutmeg
2 pints/generous 1 litre stock, made with 2 herb stock cubes
4–6 tablespoons cream
Garnish
few watercress leaves
Illustrated on page 18

28

Winter Vegetable Soup

COOKING TIME 10 minutes
PRESSURE high
SERVES 4–6

1 lb/0.5 kg potatoes
1 onion
2 leeks
2 sticks celery
2 oz/50 g butter
2 pints/generous 1 litre
 chicken stock
 or water
salt and pepper
1 bay leaf
pinch dried chervil
4 tablespoons cream

Prepare and coarsely chop the vegetables, using the green and white parts of the leeks. Heat the butter in the open cooker (with the trivet removed) and sauté all the vegetables together for 5 minutes. Add the stock, seasoning and herbs, making sure that the cooker is not more than half full. Bring to high pressure and cook for 10 minutes.

Allow the pressure to reduce at room temperature. Either press the soup through a sieve, or blend in a liquidiser, remembering to discard the bay leaf. Return to the open cooker, check the seasoning, reheat and just before serving stir in the cream.

To freeze
When cold, freeze in polythene containers, leaving a small headspace, or foil bags. Stir in the cream at the reheating stage.

Ham and Pea Soup

COOKING TIME 10 minutes
PRESSURE high
SERVES 4

4 oz/100 g streaky bacon
2 leeks
1 stick celery
1 onion
4 oz/100 g split peas
1½ pints/9 dl chicken
 stock
salt and pepper
1 bay leaf
2 tablespoons chopped
 parsley

Rind and chop the bacon; prepare and chop the leeks, celery and onion. Place the bacon pieces in the open cooker (with the trivet removed) and place over a moderate heat until the fat runs. Add the prepared vegetables and sauté for 5 minutes. Add the peas, stock, seasoning and bay leaf, making sure that the cooker is not more than half full. Bring to high pressure, on a low heat, and cook for 10 minutes.

Allow the pressure to reduce at room temperature. Remove the bay leaf, check the seasoning, stir in the chopped parsley and serve.

To freeze
When cold, freeze in polythene containers, leaving a small headspace, or foil bags.

Note
If preferred, this soup may be sieved, liquidised, or the vegetables may be mashed into the soup.

Lentil and Tomato Soup

When making soups with the pulses (lentils, split peas, etc.) in a pressure cooker, it is not necessary to soak them overnight.

Rind and chop the bacon, onion and carrot. Place the pieces of bacon in the open cooker (with the trivet removed) and put over a moderate heat until the fat runs. Add the prepared onion and carrot and sauté for 5 minutes. Stir in the lentils, tomatoes, bouquet garni, pepper and stock, making sure that the cooker is not more than half full. Bring to high pressure, on a low heat, and cook for 10 minutes.

Allow the pressure to reduce at room temperature. Check the seasoning—if you have used chicken stock it may be necessary to add a little salt; ham stock is usually sufficiently salty. Remove the bouquet garni and serve with croûtons sprinkled over the soup, or handed in a separate bowl.

To freeze
When cold, freeze in polythene containers, leaving a small headspace, or foil bags.

Note
If preferred, this soup may be sieved or liquidised, or the vegetables may be mashed into the soup.

COOKING TIME 10 minutes
PRESSURE high
SERVES 4

4 rashers streaky bacon
1 onion
1 carrot
4 oz/100 g lentils
1 small can tomatoes
bouquet garni
pepper
1½ pints/9 dl ham or
  chicken stock
croûtons to serve

Chicken and Corn Soup

Place the chicken stock, water, chicken, nutmeg, salt and pepper and sweetcorn in the cooker with the trivet removed, making sure that the cooker is not more than half full. Bring to high pressure and cook for 5 minutes.

Allow the pressure to reduce at room temperature. Check the seasoning, then stir in the chopped parsley.

COOKING TIME 5 minutes
PRESSURE high
SERVES 4–6

1 pint/6 dl chicken stock
½ pint/3 dl water
4–6 oz/100–175 g cooked
  chicken meat, chopped
pinch nutmeg
salt and pepper
1 small can sweetcorn
  kernels
2–3 tablespoons chopped
  parsley

Clear Game Soup

COOKING TIME 25 minutes
PRESSURE high
SERVES 4

2 onions
2 carrots
1–2 sticks celery
2 oz/50 g bacon fat
8 oz/225 g pie veal, cubed
carcase and left-over meat
  from 1 partridge, pheasant
  or 2 pigeons
1½ pints/9 dl water
few sprigs parsley
salt and pepper
3–4 tablespoons port or
  full-bodied red wine

Prepare and coarsely chop the onions, carrots and celery. Heat the bacon fat in the open cooker (with the trivet removed) and sauté the prepared vegetables for 5–10 minutes, until softened and just beginning to brown. Add the pie veal and sauté for a further 3–4 minutes. Break up the carcase and add to the cooker together with the water, parsley and salt and pepper, making sure that the cooker is not more than half full. Bring to high pressure and cook for 25 minutes.

Allow the pressure to reduce at room temperature. Strain the soup through a sieve lined with a piece of kitchen paper. Check the seasoning, add the wine and cook over a high heat for 2–3 minutes. Serve with fingers of toast.

To freeze
When cold, freeze in polythene containers, leaving a small headspace, or foil bags. Add the wine at the re-heating stage.

Oxtail Soup

COOKING TIME 40 minutes
PRESSURE high
SERVES 4–6

1 medium oxtail
1 tablespoon oil
2 turnips
2 onions
2 carrots
1–2 sticks celery
bouquet garni
salt and pepper
2 pints/generous 1 litre
  beef stock or water
2–3 tablespoons port or
  Burgundy

This soup should be made the day before it is required, so that the fat may be skimmed from the surface.

Ask the butcher to cut the oxtail into joints. Wash and dry the joints. Heat the oil in the open cooker (with the trivet removed) and sauté the joints until browned on all sides. Add the prepared and chopped vegetables, bouquet garni, salt and pepper and stock, making sure that the cooker is not more than half full. Bring to high pressure and cook for 40 minutes.

Allow the pressure to reduce at room temperature. Strain the soup and take the meat from the oxtail joints. Keep the soup and meat, separately, in the refrigerator overnight.

The next day, skim the fat from the surface and place the soup and pieces of meat in a pan. Bring to the boil, check the seasoning and stir in the port or Burgundy. Boil for 2–3 minutes, then serve.

If a thicker oxtail soup is preferred, whisk in small pieces of beurre manié (equal quantities of fat and flour blended together) before adding the port.

Vichyssoise

Discard the green parts of the leeks and chop the white parts. Chop the onion. Peel and cube the potatoes. Heat the butter in the open cooker (with the trivet removed) and sauté the prepared vegetables for 5 minutes, without allowing them to brown. Add the salt and pepper and stock, making sure that the cooker is not more than half full. Bring to high pressure and cook for 6 minutes.

Allow the pressure to reduce at room temperature, then either press the soup through a sieve or blend in the liquidiser. Check the seasoning and leave to chill in the refrigerator. Before serving stir in the cream and sprinkle with the chives.

To freeze
Freeze in polythene containers, leaving a headspace, or foil bags. When thawed, stir in the cream.

Note
This is a delicious cold summer soup.

COOKING TIME 6 minutes
PRESSURE high
SERVES 4

4 leeks
1 onion
2–3 small potatoes
1 oz/25 g butter
salt and pepper
1 pint/6 dl chicken stock
½ pint/3 dl single cream
2–3 tablespoons snipped chives

Fresh Green Pea Soup

Chop the spring onions and tear the lettuce leaves into shreds. Heat the butter in the open cooker (with the trivet removed) and sauté the peas, onions and lettuce for 5 minutes, without allowing them to brown. Add the stock, salt, pepper and sugar, making sure that the cooker is not more than half full. Bring to high pressure and cook for 5 minutes.

Allow the pressure to reduce at room temperature, then sieve, or blend the ingredients in the liquidiser. Reheat, check the seasoning and stir in the cream or milk, but do not allow the soup to boil. Garnish with mint. This makes a refreshing start to a summer meal.

Variation
The peas may be replaced by 1 lb (0.5 kg) shelled broad beans. Omit the sugar and add a little chopped fresh sage. Garnish with parsley or chives.

To freeze
Allow to cool, then freeze in polythene containers, leaving a small headspace, or foil containers. Add the cream or milk at the reheating stage.

COOKING TIME 5 minutes
PRESSURE high
SERVES 4–6

4 spring onions
4 outer lettuce leaves
2 oz/50 g butter
1 lb/0.5 kg fresh garden peas (weight after shelling)
1½ pints/9 dl chicken stock
salt and pepper
pinch sugar
½ pint/3 dl single cream or milk
Garnish
mint leaves

Fish

Many people forget that fish can provide a nourishing and appetising meal and is an important part of a balanced diet. There is a wide variety available, although the choice may be limited by the season and the area in which you live. Frozen fish is readily available all the year round and is good value as it is ready prepared. It is often better to purchase frozen fish unless you have a reliable wet fish shop in your area, and sadly these are fast disappearing from our high streets.

Although fish does not normally require a long cooking period by the traditional methods, there are advantages in pressure cooking fish. As a small amount of liquid is required for the cooking and the fish is cooked in steam from that liquid, the fish retains texture, flavour and nutritive value. The cooking liquid may be utilised in an accompanying sauce. I find it an advantage to wrap the fish in foil or butter papers—this also makes it easier to remove the cooked fish from

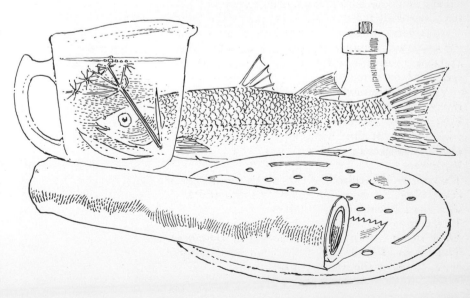

the cooker. A further advantage is that during the cooking the characteristic smell of fish does not permeate the whole house.

Garnishes are important for all dishes, but in particular for fish dishes. Lemon twists and slices or quarters are the most usual garnishes for fish, but watercress, parsley, olives, tomato, cucumber, pimentos, capers and gherkins may be used.

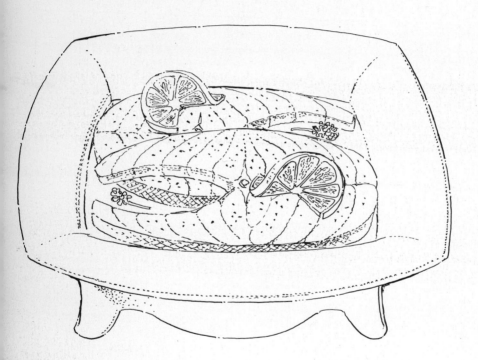

Rules for pressure cooking fish

1 Clean, trim and wash the fish. Pat dry with kitchen paper; season, sprinkle with lemon juice and herbs, and dot with butter. Wrap in foil or butter papers.

2 Pour the liquid (water, dry white wine, dry cider or fish stock) into the cooker. The amount of liquid required may be $\frac{1}{4}$ pint (1.5 dl) or $\frac{1}{2}$ pint (3 dl) depending on your model of cooker, so check with the manufacturer's leaflet.

3 Put the trivet in the base of the cooker and add the fish parcels.

4 Bring to high pressure and cook for the required time—see pages 37–8.

5 Allow the pressure to reduce with cold water.

Celery and mushroom soup (see page 26)

The cooking times will vary according to the size of the steaks, fillets or whole fish. Allow the same cooking times for frozen fish. It is not necessary to thaw frozen fish before pressure cooking.

Fish	Available	Minutes at high pressure
WHITE FISH		
Bass	May–July	Steaks 3–6 minutes Small whole fish 5–6 minutes per lb (0.5 kg)
Bream	July–December	Fillets 3–6 minutes Small whole fish 5–6 minutes per lb (0.5 kg)
Brill	All year round Best January–April	Fillets 3–6 minutes Small whole fish 5–6 minutes per lb (0.5 kg)
Cod	All year round Best October–March	Steaks and fillets 3–6 minutes
Coley	All year round	Fillets 3–6 minutes
Haddock *(fresh or* *smoked)*	All year round Best November–February	Steaks and fillets 3–6 minutes Small whole fish 5–6 minutes per lb (0.5 kg)
Hake	June–January	Fillets 3–6 minutes
Halibut	July–March	Steaks and fillets 3–6 minutes Small whole fish 5–6 minutes per lb (0.5 kg)
John Dory	September–January	Fillets 3–6 minutes
Plaice	All year round Best June–January	Fillets 3–6 minutes
Rock salmon	All year round	Steaks and fillets 3–6 minutes
Skate	October–March	Wings 3–6 minutes
Sole	All year round Best April–January	Fillets 3–6 minutes Whole fish 5–6 minutes per lb (0.5 kg)

Bacon in a hurry (see page 64)

Fish	Available	Minutes at high pressure
Turbot	All year round Best May–July	Steaks and fillets 3–6 minutes Whole fish 5–6 minutes per lb (0.5 kg)
Whiting	All year round	Steaks and fillets 4–5 minutes Whole fish 5–6 minutes per lb (0.5 kg)

The following sauces are suitable to serve with white fish–either as a coating sauce, or separately in a sauce boat: anchovy, cheese, hard-boiled egg, parsley or caper. Use the cooking liquid as part of the liquid in the sauce.

OILY FISH

Herring	All year round Best May–March	Whole fish 5–8 minutes
Mackerel	All year round	Whole fish 5–8 minutes
Mullet (grey) *(red)*	August–February May–September	Whole fish 5–8 minutes
Salmon	Best May–July	Steaks 6–8 minutes Whole fish 6 minutes per lb (0.5 kg)
Trout	All year round	Whole fish 5–8 minutes

Mustard and caper sauces go well with herring, mackerel and mullet. If serving salmon cold, accompany with mayonnaise, tartare sauce or French dressing; if serving hot, hollandaise sauce (see page 126) is the traditional accompaniment.

Curried Haddock

COOKING TIME 5 minutes
PRESSURE high
SERVES 4

1 tablespoon oil
2 onions, finely chopped
1 clove garlic, crushed
2 tablespoons curry powder
4 haddock steaks
½ pint/3 dl stock
salt and pepper
pinch thyme
6 oz/175 g long-grain rice
4 tablespoons double
  cream

Heat the oil in the open cooker (with the trivet removed) and sauté the onions and garlic for 2–3 minutes. Stir in the curry powder and cook for a further 2 minutes. Place the steaks on top of the onions, pour in the stock and add the seasoning and thyme. Place the trivet on top. Place the rice in an ovenproof bowl, add sufficient lightly salted water to come two-thirds of the way up the bowl and cover with a piece of foil. Place the bowl of rice on top of the trivet. Bring to high pressure and cook for 5 minutes.

Allow the pressure to reduce at room temperature. Fork up the rice and arrange around the edge of a serving dish. Lift out the haddock steaks and place down the centre of the dish. Stir the cream into the curry sauce, reheat, check the seasoning and pour over the fish.

Haddock in Sour Cream Sauce

COOKING TIME 4 minutes
PRESSURE high
SERVES 4

1½ lb/0.75 kg haddock
  fillets
1 onion, finely chopped
4 oz/100 g mushrooms,
  sliced
salt and pepper
squeeze lemon juice
1 oz/25 g butter
½ pint/3 dl water
Sour cream sauce
2 cartons soured cream
1 tablespoon lemon juice
salt and pepper
1 tablespoon chopped
  parsley
Garnish
paprika

Wash and dry the haddock fillets. Place on a piece of foil and sprinkle over the chopped onion, mushrooms, seasoning and lemon juice. Dot with butter. Form into a parcel.

Pour the water into the cooker and place the trivet in the bottom. Place the foil parcel on the trivet. Bring to high pressure and cook for 4 minutes.

Allow the pressure to reduce with cold water.

To make the sauce, heat the soured cream in a pan to just below boiling point. Stir in the lemon juice, seasoning to taste and chopped parsley.

Arrange the fish and vegetables on a serving dish, pour over the sauce and serve garnished with a sprinkling of paprika.

Kedgeree

Wash and dry the haddock fillets. Place on a sheet of foil, dot with half the butter and sprinkle with salt and pepper. Form into a parcel. Pour the water into the bottom of the cooker and place the trivet in the base. Place the foil parcel on the trivet. Put the rice in the solid separator and pour in the lightly salted water. Cover with a piece of foil. Place in the cooker with the fish. Bring to high pressure and cook for 5 minutes.

Reduce the pressure with cold water. Remove the fish, rice, water and trivet from the cooker. Flake the cooked fish. Heat the remaining butter in the open cooker, add the fish, rice and cream. Gently mix together and allow the cream to heat. Check the seasoning and stir in the chopped parsley. Spoon into a warm dish and serve garnished with chopped hard-boiled egg.

COOKING TIME 5 minutes
PRESSURE high
SERVES 4

1 lb/0.5 kg smoked haddock
  fillets
2 oz/50 g butter
salt and pepper
½ pint/3 dl water
4 oz/100 g long-grain rice
¼ pint/1.5 dl lightly salted
  water
¼ pint/1.5 dl single cream
2–3 tablespoons chopped
  parsley
Garnish
chopped hard-boiled egg

Spicy Cod

Wash and dry the cod steaks. Heat the butter in the open cooker (with the trivet removed) and sauté the onions, garlic and pepper for 3–4 minutes. Stir in the tomato purée, tomatoes, water or stock, basil, chilli powder, sugar and seasoning. Place the cod steaks on top. Bring to high pressure and cook for 4 minutes.

Reduce the pressure with cold water. Arrange the sauce and cod steaks on a warm serving dish. Serve garnished with chopped parsley.

COOKING TIME 4 minutes
PRESSURE high
SERVES 4

4 cod steaks
1 oz/25 g butter
2 onions, sliced
1 clove garlic, crushed
1 green pepper, seeded
  and chopped
1 teaspoon tomato purée
1 8-oz/227-g can tomatoes
¼ pint/1.5 dl water or stock
pinch basil
pinch chilli powder
2 teaspoons brown sugar
salt and pepper
Garnish
chopped parsley

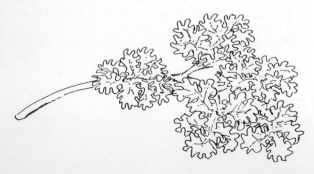

Cod in Cider

COOKING TIME 5 minutes
PRESSURE high
SERVES 4

1½ lb/0.75 kg cod fillets
1 oz/25 g butter
8 medium-sized potatoes,
  thinly sliced
8 oz/225 g leeks, sliced
1 green pepper, seeded and
  chopped
1–2 sticks celery, sliced
1 clove garlic, crushed
¼ pint/1.5 dl dry cider
pinch dried thyme
1 small can tomatoes
1 bay leaf
few stoned black olives
salt and pepper
Garnish
chopped parsley

Skin the fillets and cut into chunks. Heat the butter in the open cooker (with the trivet removed) and sauté the prepared vegetables and garlic for 3–4 minutes. Stir in the fish pieces, cider, thyme, tomatoes, bay leaf, olives and seasoning. Bring to high pressure and cook for 5 minutes.

Reduce the pressure with cold water. Discard the bay leaf, check the seasoning and spoon into a serving dish. Garnish with chopped parsley and serve with French bread and a green or mixed salad.

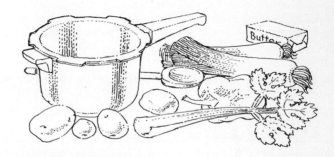

Halibut with Almonds

COOKING TIME 4 minutes
PRESSURE high
SERVES 4

4 halibut steaks
2 oz/50 g butter
salt and pepper
4 oz/100 g mushrooms,
  sliced
1 onion, chopped
4 tablespoons dry white
  wine
½ pint/3 dl water
4 oz/100 g blanched
  almonds
Garnish
sprigs of watercress

Wash and dry the halibut steaks. Place on a sheet of foil, dot with the butter and sprinkle with salt and pepper. Scatter over the mushrooms and onion, and add the wine. Form into a parcel.

Pour the water into the cooker and place the trivet in the bottom. Place the foil parcel on the trivet. Bring to high pressure and cook for 4 minutes. Brown the almonds under a moderate grill.

Allow the pressure to reduce with cold water. Arrange the fish and vegetables on a warm serving dish. Pour over the cooking liquor from the foil parcel and scatter over the almonds. Serve garnished with sprigs of watercress.

Mustard Herrings

Split and bone the herrings. Place each one on a sheet of foil. Spread with the mustard, sprinkle over the onion and season. Dot with the butter and add 2 tablespoons cream to each. Secure the parcels.

Pour the water into the cooker and place the trivet in the bottom. Place the parcels on the trivet. Bring to high pressure and cook for 6 minutes. Reduce the pressure with cold water.

Take out the parcels and place the herrings on a heated dish. Tip over the cream and cooking juices and serve garnished with lemon wedges.

COOKING TIME 6 minutes
PRESSURE high
SERVES 4

4 herrings
2 teaspoons French
 mustard
1 onion, chopped
salt and pepper
2 oz/50 g butter
¼ pint/1.5 dl single cream
½ pint/3 dl water
Garnish
lemon wedges

Herrings in White Wine

Split and bone the herrings. Heat the butter in the open cooker (with the trivet removed) and sauté the fish lightly on both sides. Remove.

Pour the wine into the cooker and put the trivet (lightly brushed with oil) in the bottom. Place the fish on the trivet. Sprinkle with salt and pepper and add the bay leaf. Bring to high pressure and cook for 5 minutes.

Reduce the pressure with cold water. Lift out the trivet and herrings, place the fish on a serving dish and keep warm. Return the open cooker to the heat and boil the wine until reduced by half. Pour over the fish and serve sprinkled with chopped parsley.

COOKING TIME 5 minutes
PRESSURE high
SERVES 4

4 herrings
2 oz/50 g butter
½ pint/3 dl dry white wine
salt and pepper
1 bay leaf
1 tablespoon chopped
 parsley

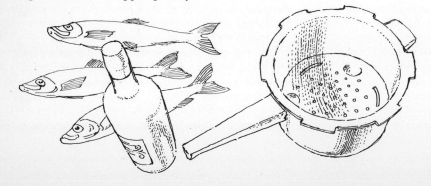

Soused Herrings

COOKING TIME 6 minutes
PRESSURE high
SERVES 6

6 herrings
salt and pepper
1 blade mace
2–3 cloves
6 peppercorns
3–4 whole allspice
1 onion, sliced
2 bay leaves
¼ pint/1.5 dl malt vinegar
¼ pint/1.5 dl water

Clean the herrings and remove the heads and tails. Split and bone them. Season each fillet with salt and pepper, and roll up from the tail end with the skin outside. Secure with a wooden cocktail stick.

Place the prepared rolled fillets in the cooker with the trivet removed. Add the mace, cloves, peppercorns, allspice, onion, bay leaves, vinegar and water. Bring to high pressure and cook for 6 minutes.

·Reduce the pressure with cold water. Allow the herrings to cool in the cooking liquor. Serve cold with a selection of salads. Soused herrings may be served as a starter or a main course.

Mackerel with Gooseberry Sauce

COOKING TIME 6 minutes
PRESSURE high
SERVES 4

4 mackerel, cleaned
salt and pepper
squeeze lemon juice
2 tablespoons chopped
  parsley
2 oz/50 g butter
½ pint/3 dl water
Gooseberry sauce
8 oz/225 g gooseberries
  or 1 8-oz/227-g can
  gooseberries
4 tablespoons water
pinch nutmeg
1 tablespoon castor sugar
1 oz/25 g butter
Garnish
watercress

Remove the heads, tails and fins from the mackerel. Make 3 or 4 diagonal slits across the top of each and sprinkle with salt, pepper, lemon juice and chopped parsley. Dot with butter and wrap each mackerel in a piece of foil.

Pour the water into the cooker and put the trivet in the bottom. Place the mackerel parcels on the trivet. Bring to high pressure and cook for 6 minutes. Reduce the pressure with cold water.

Meanwhile, prepare the sauce. Place the topped and tailed gooseberries in a pan with the water. Bring to the boil, cover and simmer until softened. (Omit this stage with canned gooseberries.) Cool slightly, then blend in the liquidiser or rub through a sieve. Reheat the purée and stir in the nutmeg, sugar and butter.

Lift the fish from the cooker. Unwrap the parcels and place the mackerel on a heated dish. Garnish with sprigs of watercress and serve the sauce separately.

To freeze

The gooseberry sauce may be frozen. Cool and pack in polythene containers, leaving a small headspace, or foil bags.

Trout with Mint

Wipe the trout inside with wet kitchen paper. Sprinkle inside and outside with seasoning. Place a sprig of mint inside each trout. Place each trout on a sheet of foil, dot with butter and sprinkle with grated lemon rind and juice. Secure the parcels.

Pour the water into the cooker and place the trivet in the bottom. Place the parcels on the trivet. Bring to high pressure and cook for 6 minutes. Reduce the pressure with cold water.

Take out the parcels and place the trout on a warm dish. Pour over the cooking juices from the foil. Serve garnished with mint leaves and lemon wedges.

COOKING TIME 6 minutes
PRESSURE high
SERVES 4

4 trout, cleaned
salt and pepper
4 sprigs fresh mint
2 oz/50 g butter
grated rind and juice of
  1 lemon
½ pint/3 dl water
Garnish
mint leaves
lemon wedges

Tuna Savoury

Place tuna (plus oil) in a bowl and flake with a fork. Grease an ovenproof dish that can be easily accommodated in your cooker and place the rice in the bottom. Cover with a layer of tuna, then the peas, seasoning each layer well. Add the lemon juice to the béchamel sauce and pour into the dish. Arrange the tomato slices on top. Cover with foil.

Pour the water into the cooker and place the trivet in the bottom. Stand the dish on the trivet. Bring to high pressure and cook for 10 minutes.

Allow the pressure to reduce at room temperature. Take out the dish, remove the foil and sprinkle the surface with grated cheese. Brown under a hot grill and serve garnished with parsley.

COOKING TIME 10 minutes
PRESSURE high
SERVES 4

1 7-oz/198-g can tuna fish
4 oz/100 g cooked long-
  grain rice
1 small packet frozen peas
salt and pepper
squeeze lemon juice
½ pint/3 dl béchamel
  sauce (see page 125)
2 tomatoes, sliced
½ pint/3 dl water
2 oz/50 g cheese, grated
Garnish
sprigs parsley

44

Bacon and bean stew (see page 65)
Oxtail stew – overleaf (see page 56)

Meat

A pressure cooker lends itself ideally to cooking pot-roasts, casseroles, braised dishes and bacon joints. Cutlets, chops, liver, kidneys and gammon rashers can be cooked in a pressure cooker, but I think with these more prime cuts there is a time saving only if you cook the accompanying vegetables at the same time in the separators.

So that the finished dish has a good, rich flavour and pot-roasts look nicely browned, the meat should be sautéed in the open cooker in hot dripping, butter or oil.

Joints may be pressure cooked from frozen, allowing 25 minutes per pound (0.5 kg). Frozen joints are a little difficult to sauté as they tend to spit (due to the water content) and only the projecting pieces brown. Cooked, frozen made-up dishes—stews, casseroles, etc.–may be reheated from the frozen state. Remove the trivet from the cooker, pour in the minimum amount of liquid (stock, wine or water) required for your cooker (check with the manufacturer's leaflet) and add the frozen block of stew (with the wrappings removed). Bring to high pressure and cook for 3–4 minutes. Re-thicken if necessary, as extra liquid has been added. Allow the pressure to reduce at room temperature. Individual portions may be reheated in the solid separator, first placing the trivet and water in the bottom of the cooker. It makes for easier reheating if individual portions of made-up dishes are frozen in the same way as soups (see page 23). The pressure in this case can be reduced with cold water.

Beef pot-roast (see page 53)

Rules for pressure cooking meat

1 When cooking joints of meat, the cooking time is calculated per pound (0.5 kg) of meat; the amount of liquid needed (stock, water or wine) is calculated according to the pressure cooking time, but should not be less than $\frac{1}{2}$ pint (3 dl). With smaller models, $\frac{1}{4}$ pint (1.5 dl) is the minimum required, so check with the manufacturer's leaflet. See also the table opposite.

2 When cooking joints of meat, suet crust puddings or savoury suet rolls and whole poultry the trivet *is* used. It is *not* used when cooking braised dishes, casseroles or stews.

3 The size of joint depends on the size of your pressure cooker. It should not be a tight fit in the cooker–this could cause the vent pipes to become blocked. In any event, to ensure even cooking throughout a whole joint, pieces weighing up to 3 lb (1.5 kg) are recommended. Joints over that weight will not cook through evenly.

4 Stews, etc. should be thickened at the end of the pressure cooking time, in the open cooker. The thickening may be blended flour (or cornflour) and water or beurre manié–equal quantities of fat and flour blended together and whisked, in small pieces, into the stew.

5 If you want to serve a selection of vegetables with a casserole, allow the pressure to reduce with cold water 4–5 minutes before the end of the cooking time. Remove the lid, place the trivet on top of the casserole, put in the separators containing the prepared and *lightly* salted vegetables – it is necessary to select vegetables which all need the same cooking time and to cut them into even-sized pieces. Replace the lid, bring back to pressure and cook for the remainder of the calculated time.

6 Be sparing with seasonings and herbs for pressure-cooked dishes.

7 When cooking semi-liquid dishes (stews, casseroles, etc.) under pressure, do not fill the cooker more than half full.

Pressure cooking times to allow per 1 lb (0.5 kg) for joints of meat

Suitable joints	Cooking time per 1 lb (0.5 kg)
Beef	
Rolled sirloin	10 minutes
Topside	12 minutes
Rolled rump	10 minutes
Brisket	12 minutes
Silverside	15 minutes
Lamb	
Leg	15 minutes
Breast (boned and rolled)	12 minutes
Pork	
Loin (boned and rolled)	15 minutes
Fillet	12 minutes
Shoulder	15 minutes
Veal	
Fillet	12 minutes
Loin	12 minutes
Shoulder (boned)	14 minutes
Breast (boned and rolled)	14 minutes
Knuckle	10 minutes
Bacon joints	12 minutes
Ox tongue	15 minutes
Frozen joints (unthawed)	25 minutes

Joints for pressure cooking should not weigh more than 3 lb (1.5 kg).

To calculate the amount of liquid required when cooking joints under pressure:

Allow ½ pint (3 dl) for first 15 minutes cooking time plus ¼ pint (1.5 dl) for every extra 15 minutes cooking time

e.g. Joint (sirloin) weighs 2½ lb (1.25 kg)

Cooking time = 25 minutes

Liquid = ¾ pint (4.5 dl)

Cider-Braised Brisket

Place the beef in a bowl. Pour over the oil and cider; add the garlic, 2 slices of orange and seasoning. Place in the refrigerator and leave to marinate for 2–3 hours, turning the joint from time to time.

Heat the butter in the open cooker (with the trivet removed). Lift the joint from the marinade, pat dry with kitchen paper and brown on all sides in the butter. Lift out the joint and place the trivet in the base of the cooker. Replace the joint on the trivet, and pour in the marinating liquid and stock. Add the onions and bouquet garni. Bring to high pressure and cook for 30 minutes.

Allow the pressure to reduce at room temperature and remove the lid. Transfer the meat to a serving dish and keep warm. Discard the bouquet garni and thicken the sauce with the cornflour blended with a little water. Bring to the boil, stirring and cook for 2–3 minutes. Check the seasoning and serve with the brisket. Use the remaining orange slices to garnish the meat.

To freeze

Any left-over brisket may be sliced, placed in a foil tray and covered with the sauce. Cover and freeze. Reheat from frozen in a moderate oven (350°F, 180°C, Gas Mark 4) for 30–35 minutes, or in the pressure cooker for 15 minutes. Add ½ pint (3 dl) water to the cooker, place the trivet in the bottom and stand the covered foil tray on the trivet. Bring to high pressure for 15 minutes. Allow the pressure to reduce at room temperature.

COOKING TIME 30 minutes, plus 2–3 hours marinating time
PRESSURE high
SERVES 4–6

2½-lb/1.25-kg piece rolled beef brisket
2 tablespoons oil
½ pint/3 dl dry cider
1 clove garlic, crushed
1 orange, sliced
salt and pepper
2 oz/50 g butter
¼ pint/1.5 dl stock
2 onions, sliced
bouquet garni
2 teaspoons cornflour

Beef Pot-Roast

COOKING TIME 24 minutes
PRESSURE high
SERVES 4–6

1 oz/25 g dripping
2-lb/1-kg piece topside
6 rashers streaky bacon
1 onion, chopped
½ pint/3 dl water
¼ pint/1.5 dl brown ale
salt and pepper
1 tablespoon vinegar
potatoes
leeks
Brussels sprouts
1 tablespoon cornflour
Illustrated on page 48

Heat the dripping in the open cooker and brown the meat on all sides. Lift out and place the trivet in the base of the cooker. Arrange the bacon rashers and onion on the trivet, then replace the meat. Add the water, ale, seasoning and vinegar. Bring to high pressure and cook for 20 minutes.

Allow the pressure to reduce at room temperature. Remove the lid and arrange the prepared vegetables in groups around the meat—making sure that the potatoes and leeks are cut quite small so that they will cook in the same time as the sprouts. Replace the lid, return to the heat and bring to high pressure. Cook for 4 minutes.

Allow the pressure to reduce at room temperature. Lift out the meat and place on a serving dish. Surround with the vegetables and keep warm.

Take out the trivet and bacon. Return the open cooker to the heat and thicken the cooking liquor with the cornflour blended with 2 tablespoons cold water. Check the seasoning and strain into a sauce boat.

To freeze

Any left-over topside may be sliced, placed in a foil tray and covered with the gravy. Cover and freeze. Reheat from frozen in a moderate oven (350°F, 180°C, Gas Mark 4) for 30–35 minutes, or in the pressure cooker (see page 49).

Italian Pot-Roast

COOKING TIME 30 minutes
PRESSURE high
SERVES 4–6

2 tablespoons oil
2½-lb/1.25-kg piece topside
2 onions, sliced
1 clove garlic, crushed
salt and pepper
1 8-oz/227-g can tomatoes
pinch mixed herbs
½ pint/3 dl stock or water
4 tablespoons red wine
6–8 stuffed olives, sliced

Heat the oil in the cooker (with the trivet removed) and brown the joint on all sides. Lift out the joint and place the trivet in the base of the cooker. Replace the joint on the trivet. Add the onions, garlic, seasoning, tomatoes and herbs. Pour in the stock and wine, making sure that the cooker is not more than half full. Bring to high pressure and cook for 30 minutes.

Allow the pressure to reduce at room temperature. Check the seasoning, stir in the olives and serve.

To freeze

Any left-over topside may be sliced and placed in a foil dish with the remaining vegetables. Moisten with some of the cooking liquid. Cover and freeze. Reheat from frozen as recipe above.

Beef Ragoût

Trim the beef and cut into cubes. Coat lightly in a little seasoned flour. Heat the oil in the cooker (with the trivet removed) and sauté the pieces of meat until browned on all sides. Add the prepared vegetables and garlic, and sauté for a further 3–4 minutes. Stir in the seasoning, paprika, Worcestershire sauce, stock, red wine and tomato purée, making sure that the cooker is not more than half full. Add the bay leaf, bring to high pressure and cook for 15 minutes.

Allow the pressure to reduce at room temperature. Discard the bay leaf, check the seasoning and thicken if necessary with blended flour or cornflour or equal quantities of butter and flour blended together.

To freeze
Allow to cool, then pack in polythene containers.

COOKING TIME 15 minutes
PRESSURE high
SERVES 4–6

2 lb/1 kg stewing beef
seasoned flour
1 tablespoon oil
1 onion, sliced
3–4 carrots, sliced
3–4 sticks celery, sliced
2 tomatoes, sliced
1 clove garlic, crushed
salt and pepper
pinch paprika pepper
1 teaspoon Worcestershire
  sauce
½ pint/3 dl stock or water
½ pint/3 dl red wine
1 tablespoon tomato purée
1 bay leaf

Beef with Olives

Trim the beef if necessary and cut into strips. Heat the butter in the open cooker (with the trivet removed) and sauté the meat until browned on all sides. Add the bacon and sauté for a further 3–4 minutes. Add the brandy and when heated ignite it. Shake the cooker backwards and forwards until the flames die down. Add the bouquet garni, garlic, onions, carrot and seasoning. Pour in the red wine and stock, making sure that the cooker is not more than half full. Bring to high pressure and cook for 20 minutes.

Allow the pressure to reduce at room temperature. Remove the bouquet garni, check the seasoning and add the rinsed olives. Return the open cooker to the heat for 3–4 minutes to allow the olives to heat through. Serve with rice.

To freeze
Allow to cool and pack in polythene containers or foil bags. Add the olives at the reheating stage.

COOKING TIME 20 minutes
PRESSURE high
SERVES 4–6

2 lb/1 kg beef skirt
2 oz/50 g butter
2–3 rashers back bacon,
  chopped
3–4 tablespoons brandy
bouquet garni
1 clove garlic, crushed
2 onions, sliced
1 carrot, sliced
salt and pepper
¼ pint/1.5 dl red wine
½ pint/3 dl stock or water
4 oz/100 g stoned black
  olives

54

Hungarian Goulash

COOKING TIME 20 minutes
PRESSURE high
SERVES 4

1½ lb/0.75 kg chuck steak
seasoned flour
1 tablespoon oil
3 onions, sliced
2–4 teaspoons paprika
1 teaspoon vinegar
pinch caraway seeds
1 15-oz/425-g can tomatoes
½ pint/3 dl stock or water
pinch sugar
salt and pepper
pinch marjoram
3 tablespoons soured cream

Trim the beef and cut into cubes and lightly coat with seasoned flour. Heat the oil in the cooker (with the trivet removed) and sauté the meat until browned on all sides. Add the onions and sauté for a further 3–4 minutes. Blend the paprika with the vinegar and add to the meat together with the caraway seeds, tomatoes, stock, sugar, salt, pepper and marjoram, making sure that the cooker is not more than half full. Bring to high pressure and cook for 20 minutes.

Allow the pressure to reduce at room temperature. Check the seasoning and stir in the soured cream. Serve with buttered noodles or tagliatelli. A crisp green salad is a good accompaniment to goulash.

To freeze

Allow to cool, then pack in polythene containers or foil bags. Stir in the cream when reheated.

Mexican Beef

COOKING TIME 15 minutes,
  plus 1 hour for soaking
  beans
PRESSURE high
SERVES 4

8 oz/225 g red kidney
  beans
2 oz/50 g butter
1 onion, sliced
1 green pepper, seeded
  and sliced
1 lb/0.5 kg minced beef
1 clove garlic, crushed
1 8-oz/227-g can tomatoes
pinch sugar
salt and pepper
3–4 teaspoons chilli
  powder
1 bay leaf
½ pint/3 dl beef stock

Place the beans in a bowl, cover with cold water and leave to soak for 1 hour.

Heat the butter in the open cooker (with the trivet removed) and sauté the prepared vegetables for 5 minutes. Add the minced beef and cook until browned. Add the drained beans, garlic, tomatoes, sugar, seasoning, chilli powder and bay leaf. Pour in the stock, making sure that the cooker is not more than half full. Bring to high pressure and cook for 15 minutes.

Allow the pressure to reduce at room temperature. Discard the bay leaf. Check the seasoning and serve with pasta or rice.

To freeze

Allow to cool, then pack in polythene containers or foil bags.

Stuffed Cabbage Leaves

Cut away the hard stem from each cabbage leaf. Blanch the leaves in boiling salted water for 2 minutes. Drain and pat dry on kitchen paper.

Heat the butter in the open cooker (with the trivet removed) and sauté the chopped onion and minced beef for 5 minutes. Mix in the breadcrumbs, seasoning, herbs, Tabasco sauce and sultanas. Spoon the mixture into a bowl. When cool, spread a portion of the mixture on each cabbage leaf. Make parcels and secure each with a wooden cocktail stick.

Put the trivet in the base of the cooker and place the cabbage parcels on the trivet. Pour in the tomatoes and stock, making sure that the cooker is not more than half full. Bring to high pressure and cook for 15 minutes.

Allow the pressure to reduce at room temperature. Remove the cocktail sticks from the cabbage parcels. Arrange the parcels on a serving dish. Taste the sauce and add a pinch of sugar if necessary and either pour over the cabbage parcels, or serve separately.

COOKING TIME 15 minutes
PRESSURE high
SERVES 4

8–10 large cabbage leaves
1 oz/25 g butter
1 onion, chopped
12 oz/350 g minced beef
4 oz/100 g fresh white
  breadcrumbs
salt and pepper
pinch mixed herbs
few drops Tabasco sauce
1 tablespoon sultanas
1 15-oz/425-g can tomatoes
½ pint/3 dl stock or water

Oxtail Stew

Trim the excess fat from the pieces of oxtail. Season the flour with salt and pepper and use to coat the pieces of oxtail. Heat the oil in the open cooker (with the trivet removed) and sauté the oxtail until browned on both sides. Add the prepared vegetables and sauté for a further 3–4 minutes. Add the bouquet garni, stock, wine and tomato purée blended with the Worcestershire sauce, making sure that the cooker is not more than half full. Bring to high pressure and cook for 40 minutes.

Allow the pressure to reduce at room temperature. Skim off the surplus fat by drawing a piece of kitchen paper across the surface. Discard the bouquet garni, check the seasoning and thicken, if liked.

If convenient, it is a good idea to prepare this dish in advance, so that the fat can be skimmed off.

To freeze

Allow to cool and pack in polythene containers. Reheat from frozen in a moderate oven (350°F, 180°C, Gas Mark 4) for 40 minutes, or in the pressure cooker.

COOKING TIME 40 minutes
PRESSURE high
SERVES 4

1 oxtail, jointed
2 tablespoons flour
salt and pepper
1 tablespoon oil
3 onions, sliced
3 sticks celery, chopped
2 leeks, sliced
4 carrots, sliced
bouquet garni
¾ pint/4.5 dl stock or water
¼ pint/1.5 dl red wine
1 tablespoon tomato purée
1 tablespoon Worcestershire
  sauce
Illustrated on pages 46–7

56

Chicken provençale (see page 71)

Traditional Steak and Kidney Pudding

COOKING TIME 15 minutes
at high pressure for filling
15 minutes pre-steaming
25 minutes at low pressure
for complete pudding
SERVES 4

Filling
12 oz/350 g chuck steak
4 oz/100 g kidney
seasoned flour
1 onion, chopped
4 oz/100 g mushrooms,
  sliced
1 bay leaf
½ pint/3 dl stock or water
Suet pastry
8 oz/225 g self-raising
  flour
pinch salt
pinch mixed herbs
4 oz/110 g shredded suet
cold water to mix

2½ pints/1.25 litres boiling
water

Trim and cut the steak into cubes. Skin, core and slice the kidney. Toss the prepared steak and kidney in a little seasoned flour. Place in the cooker (with the trivet removed) and add the onion, mushrooms, bay leaf and stock, making sure that the cooker is not more than half full. Bring to high pressure and cook for 15 minutes. Allow the pressure to reduce at room temperature.

Meanwhile, make the suet pastry. Sieve the flour and salt into a bowl. Mix in the herbs and suet. Mix in sufficient cold water to form a soft dough. Roll out two-thirds and use to line a 1½-pint (1-litre) greased pudding basin made of china, ovenproof glass or foil.

Allow the meat mixture to cool, discard the bay leaf and ladle into the lined basin with half the cooking liquid. Roll out the remaining dough to make a lid and use to cover the pudding, dampening the edges for a secure seal. Cover securely with a piece of foil, making a pleat in the foil to allow room for the suet crust to rise during cooking.

Wash the pressure cooker, place the trivet in the base and pour in the boiling water. Stand the basin on the trivet. Put the lid on the cooker and when steam escapes through the vent in the lid, lower the heat and steam (without the pressure weight) for 15 minutes. (This pre-steaming makes the suet pastry light.) Increase the heat, bring to low pressure and cook for 25 minutes.

Allow the pressure to reduce at room temperature. Remove the basin from the cooker, take off the foil and serve from the basin, which may be wrapped in a napkin. Serve with the gravy remaining from cooking the meat.

Traditional beef curry (see page 97)

59

Lamb Carbonnade

Cut the lamb into cubes and lightly coat in seasoned flour. Heat the butter in the cooker (with the trivet removed) and sauté the lamb for 3–4 minutes. Add the prepared onions and garlic and sauté for a further 5 minutes. Add the ale, seasoning and bouquet garni. Bring to high pressure and cook for 15 minutes.

Allow the pressure to reduce at room temperature. Check the seasoning, discard the bouquet garni and serve with French bread, potatoes or pasta.

COOKING TIME 15 minutes
PRESSURE high
SERVES 4

1½ lb/0.75 kg leg of lamb
seasoned flour
2 oz/50 g butter
1 lb/0.5 kg onions, sliced
1 clove garlic, crushed
½ pint/3 dl brown ale
salt and pepper
bouquet garni

Peppered Lamb Stew with Dumplings

Lightly coat the trimmed pieces of middle neck in seasoned flour. Heat the dripping in the cooker (with the trivet removed) and brown the meat on all sides. Add the prepared vegetables and sauté for a further 3–4 minutes. Add the stock and Worcestershire sauce, making sure that the cooker is not more than half full. Bring to high pressure and cook for 15 minutes.

Meanwhile, mix the ingredients together for the dumplings – the mixture should be a fairly soft dough – and form into eight even-sized balls.

Allow the pressure to reduce at room temperature and remove the lid. Return the open cooker to the heat and bring the liquid to the boil. Add the dumplings, cover with a large plate and simmer for 10 minutes. Check the seasoning and serve.

To freeze
Allow to cool and freeze in polythene containers. Prepare and add the dumplings at the reheating stage.

COOKING TIME 15 minutes, plus 10 minutes for the dumplings
PRESSURE high
SERVES 4

2 lb/1 kg middle neck of lamb
seasoned flour
1 oz/25 g dripping
2 onions, sliced
3 carrots, sliced
1 small turnip, cubed
¾ pint/4.5 dl stock or water
1–2 tablespoons Worcestershire sauce
Savoury dumplings
4 oz/100 g self-raising flour
2 oz/50 g shredded suet
1 small onion, grated
pinch mixed herbs
pinch salt
4 tablespoons cold water

Spicy Lamb and Aubergines

COOKING TIME 15 minutes
PRESSURE high
SERVES 4

2 aubergines
salt and pepper
1 oz/25 g butter
2 lb/1 kg raw lamb, minced
1 onion, chopped
3 teaspoons curry powder
2 tablespoons curry paste
2–3 teaspoons Worcester-
  shire sauce
3 oz/75 g raisins
2 tablespoons chutney
½ pint/3 dl stock or water
Garnish
salted peanuts

Slice the aubergines, sprinkle with salt and leave to stand.

Heat the butter in the cooker (with the trivet removed) and brown the minced lamb. Add the onion and cook for a further 5 minutes. Stir in the curry powder, salt, pepper, curry paste, Worcestershire sauce, raisins and chutney. Rinse the aubergines and stir into the ingredients in the cooker. Pour in the stock, making sure that the cooker is not more than half full. Bring to high pressure and cook for 15 minutes.

Allow the pressure to reduce at room temperature, check the seasoning and serve the spicy lamb, garnished with salted peanuts, with a selection of side dishes—cucumber slices in natural yogurt or soured cream; tomato and onion slices; peach or mango chutney.

Devilled Lamb Chops

COOKING TIME 10 minutes
PRESSURE high
SERVES 4

2 oz/50 g butter
8 lamb cutlets
2 teaspoons dry mustard
pinch cayenne pepper
salt and pepper
2 teaspoons Worcestershire
  sauce
¼ pint/1.5 dl stock or water
¼ pint/1.5 dl dry white
  wine
2 teaspoons cornflour
¼ pint/1.5 dl cream

Heat the butter in the open cooker (with the trivet removed) and brown the lamb cutlets on each side. Blend the mustard, cayenne pepper, seasoning and Worcestershire sauce with some of the stock. Add to the cooker together with the remaining stock and the wine. Bring to high pressure and cook for 10 minutes.

Allow the pressure to reduce at room temperature. Remove the lid and arrange the chops on a serving dish and keep warm. Return the open cooker to the heat and thicken the sauce with the blended cornflour. Stir in the cream (without allowing the mixture to re-boil), check the seasoning and pour over the cutlets.

Pot-Roast of Pork with Herbs

Strip the skin from the pork and season with salt and pepper. Press the herbs into the skin. Prepare and chop the vegetables. Heat the oil in the open cooker and brown the joint on all sides and at each end. Remove. Add the vegetables and sauté until lightly browned. Remove the vegetables.

Place the trivet in the base of the cooker and put the joint on top. Pour in the stock or water, bring to high pressure and cook for 32 minutes. Allow the pressure to reduce at room temperature. Remove the lid, place the sautéed vegetables around the meat and replace the lid. Bring back to high pressure and cook for a further 5 minutes.

Allow the pressure to reduce at room temperature. Place the meat on a serving dish and surround with the vegetables. Remove the trivet and thicken the liquid in the open cooker. Serve separately.

To freeze

Any left-over pork and vegetables may be frozen. Slice the pork and place in a foil dish with the vegetables. Pour over a little unthickened stock to cover the meat slices. Cover and freeze. Reheat from frozen in a moderate oven (350°F, 180°C, Gas Mark 4) for 30–35 minutes, or in the pressure cooker (see page 49).

COOKING TIME 37 minutes
PRESSURE high
SERVES 4–6

2½-lb/1.25-kg piece boned
  and rolled loin of pork
salt and pepper
fresh rosemary and thyme
2 leeks
4–6 potatoes
2 turnips
4 carrots
2 sticks celery
1 tablespoon oil
¾ pint/4.5 dl stock or
  water
Illustrated on the jacket

Oriental Pork Chops

Remove the excess fat from the chops. Season the chops with salt and pepper. Heat the butter in the open cooker and fry the chops for 3–4 minutes on each side, until nicely browned. Remove the chops and place the trivet in the base of the cooker. Sprinkle with the 4 tablespoons rice. Add the onion slices and pieces of pepper. Arrange the chops on top and pour in the stock, making sure that the cooker is not more than half full. Bring to high pressure and cook for 10 minutes.

Allow the pressure to reduce with cold water. Arrange the chops on a serving dish. Serve with a mixed salad.

COOKING TIME 10 minutes
PRESSURE high
SERVES 4

4 loin pork chops
salt and pepper
2 oz/50 g butter
4 tablespoons uncooked
  long-grain rice
1 onion, sliced
1 green pepper, seeded and
  chopped
½ pint/3 dl stock or water

Hawaiian Pork

COOKING TIME 25 minutes
PRESSURE high
SERVES 4

1½ lb/0.75 kg pork shoulder
1 oz/25 g butter
1 onion, sliced
1 green pepper, chopped
¼ pint/1.5 dl pineapple
  juice (from canned pineapple)
¼ pint/1.5 dl stock or water
4 tablespoons vinegar
2 oz/50 g brown sugar
1 tablespoon soy sauce
salt and pepper
1 1-lb/450-g can pine-
  apple chunks
2 tablespoons cornflour

Trim the fat from the pork and cut the meat into cubes. Heat the butter in the open cooker (with the trivet removed) and sauté the pieces of pork until browned. Add the onion and green pepper and sauté for a further 3–4 minutes. Add the pineapple juice, stock, vinegar, brown sugar, soy sauce, salt and pepper, making sure that the cooker is not more than half full. Bring to high pressure and cook for 25 minutes.

Allow the pressure to reduce at room temperature. Add the drained pineapple chunks, return the open cooker to the heat and cook for 3–4 minutes, until the pineapple is heated through. Blend the cornflour with a little water and, stirring, add to the cooker. Cook for 2–3 minutes, stirring. Check the seasoning and serve with rice or noodles.

To freeze
Omit the thickening, allow to cool and pack in poly-thene containers or foil bags. Thicken with blended cornflour just before serving, as above.

Veal Marengo

COOKING TIME 12 minutes
PRESSURE high
SERVES 4

1½ lb/0.75 kg pie veal
flour
salt and pepper
¼ teaspoon thyme
2 tablespoons oil
2 onions, sliced
1 clove garlic, crushed
4 oz/100 g button mush-
  rooms
2 sprigs parsley
1 bay leaf
1 small can tomatoes
pinch sugar
½ pint/3 dl stock or water
3 tablespoons dry white wine

Trim the veal and cut into cubes. Mix together the flour, salt, pepper and thyme and lightly coat the veal pieces.

Heat the oil in the open cooker (with the trivet re-moved) and brown the veal pieces. Add the prepared onions, garlic and whole mushrooms and sauté for a further 3–4 minutes. Add the parsley, bay leaf, tomatoes and sugar. Stir in the stock and wine, making sure that the cooker is not more than half full. Bring to high pressure and cook for 12 minutes.

Allow the pressure to reduce at room temperature. Discard the parsley and bay leaf, check the seasoning and serve. If liked, thicken the liquid with the remaining seasoned flour blended with water.

To freeze
Allow to cool and pack in polythene containers or foil bags.

Veal and Caraway Roll

To make the pastry, sieve the flour and salt into a bowl. Stir in the suet and caraway seeds. Mix in sufficient cold water to form a soft dough. Turn onto a floured board and roll out to a rectangle a little narrower than the base of the cooker.

To make the filling, heat the butter in a frying pan and sauté the onion and garlic for 3–4 minutes. Off the heat, mix in the remaining ingredients. Allow to cool, then spread over the rolled out dough to within 1 inch (2.5 cm) of the edges. Roll up, as for a Swiss roll, starting from one of the short sides; pinch the ends and seam together to seal. Wrap *loosely*, but securely, in a sheet of greased foil.

Place the trivet in the base of the cooker and pour in the water. Put in the roll, put the lid on the cooker and when steam escapes through the vent in the lid, lower the heat and steam (without the pressure weight) for 20 minutes. (This pre-steaming makes the suet pastry light.) Increase the heat, bring to low pressure and cook for 35 minutes.

Allow the pressure to reduce at room temperature. Lift out the roll and transfer to a serving dish. Serve cut in slices with a tomato, mushroom or onion sauce (see pages 124 and 125) if liked.

COOKING TIME 35 minutes, plus 20 minutes pre-steaming time
PRESSURE low
SERVES 4–6

Suet pastry
8 oz/225 g self-raising flour
pinch salt
4 oz/110 g shredded suet
½ teaspoon caraway seeds
Filling
1 oz/25 g butter
1 onion, chopped
1 clove garlic, crushed
1 lb/450 g veal, minced
1 oz/25 g fresh white breadcrumbs
1 oz/25 g walnuts, chopped
1 oz/25 g sultanas
salt and pepper
3 pints/1.5 litres boiling water

Bacon in a Hurry

Place the joint in the cooker, cover with cold water and bring slowly to the boil. Remove from the heat and drain.

Place the blanched bacon joint on the trivet in the base of the cooker and add the prepared whole vegetables. Add the bay leaf, cloves, peppercorns and the stock. Bring to high pressure and cook for 30 minutes.

Allow the pressure to reduce at room temperature. Remove the joint from the cooker, strip off the skin and press the breadcrumbs into the fat. Place on a serving dish. Serve hot, or cold garnished with salad vegetables and hard-boiled eggs.

COOKING TIME 30 minutes
PRESSURE high
SERVES 4

2½-lb/1.25-kg collar joint
1 onion
1 carrot
1 leek
1 bay leaf
2 cloves
3–4 peppercorns
1 pint/6 dl stock or water
toasted breadcrumbs
Illustrated on page 36

Bacon Cassoulet

COOKING TIME 30 minutes
PRESSURE high
SERVES 4

2½-lb/1.25-kg collar or
  forehock bacon joint
2 oz/50 g butter
2 carrots
2 onions
2–3 sticks celery
4 oz/100 g haricot beans
2 tablespoons tomato purée
1 clove garlic, crushed
2–4 oz/50–100 g garlic
  sausage, thickly sliced
pepper
bouquet garni
¾ pint/4.5 dl dry white
  wine or dry cider

Place the joint in a pan, cover with cold water and bring slowly to the boil. Remove from the heat and drain.

Discard the rind from the blanched joint and cut the bacon into cubes. Heat the butter in the open cooker and sauté the bacon for 2–3 minutes. Add the prepared and sliced vegetables and sauté for a further 3–4 minutes. Add the haricot beans, tomato purée, garlic, garlic sausage, pepper and bouquet garni. Pour in the wine or cider, bring to high pressure and cook for 30 minutes.

Allow the pressure to reduce at room temperature. Check the seasoning, discard the bouquet garni and serve sprinkled with plenty of chopped parsley. Serve with hot crusty French bread.

Bacon and Bean Stew

COOKING TIME 20 minutes
PRESSURE high
SERVES 4

1½-lb/0.75-kg piece
  unsmoked bacon collar
  or slipper joint
8 oz/225 g leeks
1½ oz/40 g butter
1 onion, chopped
4 carrots, sliced
1 pint/6 dl stock
pepper
1 7½-oz/212-g can butter
  beans
2 tablespoons flour
1 tablespoon chopped
  parsley
Illustrated on page 45

Discard the rind and any excess fat from the bacon and cut the meat into cubes. Place in the cooker (with the trivet removed) and cover with cold water. Bring slowly to the boil, then drain and dry on kitchen paper.

Trim, wash and slice the leeks. Heat the butter in the open cooker and sauté the prepared vegetables for 3–4 minutes. Add the bacon cubes, stock and pepper, making sure that the cooker is not more than half full. Bring to high pressure and cook for 20 minutes.

Allow the pressure to reduce at room temperature. Return the open cooker to the heat, add the drained butter beans and allow them to heat through. Thicken the stew with the flour blended to a smooth paste with a little cold water. Check the seasoning, stir in the chopped parsley and spoon into a warmed serving dish.

Savoury Bacon Pudding

Place the bacon, beef, breadcrumbs, seasoning, mustard and parsley in a bowl. Mix in the lightly beaten egg and pineapple juice to form a fairly soft mixture. Brush the inside of a 2-pint (1.25-litre) pudding basin with oil and pack in the mixture. Cover with a piece of greaseproof paper or foil, and secure firmly under the top edge.

Place the trivet in the base of the cooker and pour in 1 pint (6 dl) water. Stand the pudding basin on the trivet. Bring to high pressure and cook for 35 minutes.

Allow the pressure to reduce at room temperature. Meanwhile, place the pineapple rings and remaining juice in a frying pan. Add the sugar and cook over a moderate heat until the pineapple rings become glazed.

Turn the pudding onto a serving dish and garnish with the glazed pineapple rings and sprigs of parsley or watercress.

COOKING TIME 35 minutes
PRESSURE high
SERVES 4

12 oz/350 g bacon, minced
4 oz/100 g beef, minced
3 oz/75 g fresh white
  breadcrumbs
1 teaspoon dry mustard
2–3 tablespoons parsley
1 egg
2 tablespoons pineapple
  juice (from the can)
1 pint/6 dl water
1 small can pineapple rings
1 tablespoon brown sugar

Tongue with Mustard Sauce

Place the tongue in a bowl, cover with cold water and leave to soak for 2 hours.

Lift out the tongue and place in the cooker with the trivet removed. Slice the carrots lengthways, coarsely chop the celery and stick the cloves into the peeled onion. Put the vegetables in the cooker with the tongue. Add the peppercorns, parsley and bay leaf and enough water to half fill the pressure cooker. Bring to high pressure and cook for 37 minutes.

Allow the pressure to reduce at room temperature. Lift the tongue onto a board and when cool enough to handle, remove the skin, gristle and small bones. Cut into slices and place on a serving dish. Spoon over 1 tablespoon of the cooking liquor, cover with foil and keep warm while making the sauce.

To make the sauce, melt the butter in a pan, add the flour and cook for 2 minutes, stirring. Gradually add the milk and cooking liquor, stirring. Bring to the boil and simmer for 2–3 minutes. Blend the mustard powder with the vinegar and add to the sauce; add pepper to taste. Serve either poured over the tongue slices, or separately.

COOKING TIME 37 minutes,
  plus 2 hours soaking time
PRESSURE high
SERVES 6

2½-lb/1.25-kg ox tongue
2 carrots
3 sticks celery
3 cloves
1 onion
10–12 peppercorns
few sprigs parsley
1 bay leaf
Mustard sauce
¾ oz/20 g butter
¾ oz/20 g flour
½ pint/3 dl milk
¼ pint/1.5 dl cooking
  liquor from tongue
2–3 teaspoons dry mustard
2 teaspoons wine vinegar
pinch pepper

66

Poultry and Game

Whole poultry and game as well as joints and casserole dishes can be cooked under pressure. If you are cooking older game and boiling fowls, then you must allow longer cooking times than for roasting chicken and young game. Venison and rabbit are both particularly good candidates for pressure cooking. Venison benefits from marinating before cooking.

Whole poultry and game need to be trussed before pressure cooking and stuffed poultry should be weighed after stuffing and the cooking time and liquid calculated accordingly.

I think the flavour of poultry is infinitely better if it is first sealed in hot butter or oil in the open cooker. This also gives the poultry an appetising appearance. There is nothing more off-putting, especially to young children, than white-looking poultry.

Whole birds weighing up to $3\frac{1}{2}$ lb (1.5 kg) are re-commended for pressure cooking to ensure that they cook evenly throughout. Whole poultry and game must not be a tight fit in the cooker, otherwise the steam may not be able to circulate freely and the vent pipes could become blocked.

Frozen poultry (whole and joints) must be fully thawed before being cooked. If cooked from the frozen state there is the danger that the calculated cooking time would not be sufficient to render harmless any bacteria there may be in the poultry.

I do not consider it an advantage to cook the smaller, young game birds (grouse, pigeons) in a pressure cooker. However, it is worth using a pressure cooker to casserole older ones.

When cooking poultry and game the cooking liquid may be water, red or white wine, dry cider or stock. The minimum amount of liquid required will depend on your type of cooker, but will be either $\frac{1}{4}$ pint (1.5 dl) or $\frac{1}{2}$ pint (3 dl) for up to 20 minutes cooking time.

Poultry or game	Cooking times at high pressure
Chicken	
Very young (poussin), halved	7 minutes
joints	4 minutes
Roasting, whole	5 minutes per lb (0.5 kg)
joints	5 minutes
Boiling, whole	10 minutes per lb (0.5 kg)
joints	10 minutes
Turkey, joints (whole turkeys are too large for pressure cookers)	10 minutes
Duck, whole	12–15 minutes per lb (0.5 kg)
joints	12 minutes
Hare, joints	40 minutes
Rabbit, joints	15 minutes
Partridge, whole	7–10 minutes (depending on age)
joints	5–7 minutes (depending on age)
Pheasant, whole	7–10 minutes (depending on age)
joints	5–7 minutes (depending on age)
Venison	20 minutes
Grouse and pigeons (older birds)	10 minutes

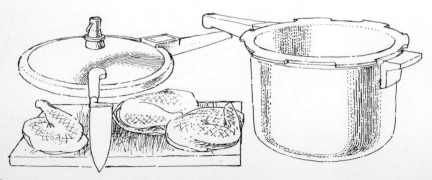

Chicken with Walnuts

COOKING TIME 7 minutes
PRESSURE high
SERVES 4

2 oz/50 g butter
4 chicken joints
2 carrots, sliced
1–2 leeks, sliced
8 small onions, peeled
pinch thyme
salt and pepper
½ pint/3 dl stock
4 oz/100 g walnuts,
  coarsely chopped

Heat the butter in the open cooker (with the trivet removed) and sauté the chicken joints until browned on all sides. Add the prepared vegetables and sauté for a further 3–4 minutes. Add the thyme, salt and pepper and pour in the stock, making sure that the cooker is not more than half full. Bring to high pressure and cook for 7 minutes.

Reduce the pressure with cold water. Arrange the chicken joints on a serving dish, spoon over the cooking liquor and arrange the vegetables around the chicken. Sprinkle with chopped walnuts.

Chicken Chasseur

COOKING TIME 7 minutes
PRESSURE high
SERVES 4

2 oz/50 g butter
4 chicken joints
1–2 tablespoons brandy
bouquet garni
salt and pepper
2 tablespoons tomato purée
¼ pint/1.5 dl stock or water
¼ pint/1.5 dl dry white
  wine

Heat the butter in the open cooker (with the trivet removed) and sauté the chicken joints until browned on all sides. Pour in the brandy, heat and ignite. Shake the cooker backwards and forwards until the flames die down. Add the bouquet garni, seasoning and tomato purée blended with the liquid, making sure that the cooker is not more than half full. Bring to high pressure and cook for 7 minutes.

Reduce the pressure with cold water. Arrange the chicken joints on a serving dish and spoon over the cooking liquor, discarding the bouquet garni.

Chicken with Rosemary

A pressure cooker is ideal for cooking poultry and meat casseroles. It is better to sauté the poultry or meat in heated oil first in the open cooker.

Peel the onion and insert the cloves. Put into the cavity of the chicken together with the rosemary. Heat the butter in the open cooker (with the trivet removed) and sauté the chicken until browned on all sides. Remove the chicken and replace the trivet in the base of the cooker. Replace the chicken on the trivet and sprinkle with salt and pepper. Pour in the stock and wine. Bring to high pressure and cook for 15 or 30 minutes, depending on the type of chicken.

Reduce the pressure with cold water. Lift out the chicken, place on a serving dish and keep warm.

To make the sauce, heat the butter in a pan, stir in the flour and cook for 2–3 minutes, stirring. Gradually stir in $\frac{1}{4}$ pint (1.5 dl) of the cooking liquor and cook until a smooth sauce is obtained. Stir in the cream, seasoning and lemon juice, reheat, but do not allow the sauce to boil. Serve with the chicken.

COOKING TIME 15 minutes
  (roasting chicken);
  30 minutes (boiling fowl)
PRESSURE high
SERVES 4
1 onion
4 cloves
few sprigs rosemary
2 oz/50 g butter
1 3-lb/1.5-kg chicken
salt and pepper
$\frac{1}{4}$ pint/1.5 dl stock
$\frac{1}{4}$ pint/1.5 dl dry white wine
Sauce
1 oz/25 g butter
1 oz/25 g flour
$\frac{1}{4}$ pint/1.5 dl double cream
juice of $\frac{1}{2}$ lemon

Chicken Provençale

COOKING TIME 7 minutes
PRESSURE high
SERVES 4

2 tablespoons oil
4 chicken joints
salt and pepper
¼ teaspoon basil
1 clove garlic, crushed
1 onion, chopped
4 oz/100 g button
  mushrooms
1 small can tomatoes
¼ pint/1.5 dl dry white wine
  or stock
¼ pint/1.5 dl stock
2 oz/50 g stuffed olives
pinch sugar
1 tablespoon cornflour
Illustrated on page 57

Heat the oil in the open cooker (with the trivet removed) and sauté the chicken portions until browned on all sides. Sprinkle with salt, pepper and basil. Add the garlic, onion, mushrooms, tomatoes, wine and stock, making sure that the cooker is not more than half full. Bring to high pressure and cook for 7 minutes.

Reduce the pressure with cold water. Lift out the chicken, place on a serving dish and keep warm. Return the open cooker to the heat and stir in the olives. Cook for 2–3 minutes to allow the olives to heat through. Check the seasoning, adding a pinch of sugar, and thicken the sauce with the cornflour blended with a little water. Spoon over the chicken.

Chicken Paprika

COOKING TIME 7 minutes
PRESSURE high
SERVES 4

2 oz/50 g butter
4 chicken joints
2 large onions, sliced
1 clove garlic, crushed
1 4-oz/100-g gammon
  rasher, cubed
salt and pepper
½ pint/3 dl stock
1½–2 tablespoons paprika
  pepper
¼ pint/1.5 double cream

Heat the butter in the open cooker (with the trivet removed) and sauté the chicken joints until browned on all sides. Remove. Sauté the onions, garlic and cubed gammon for 3–4 minutes. Replace the chicken joints and add the seasoning and stock blended with the paprika, making sure that the cooker is not more than half full. Bring to high pressure and cook for 7 minutes.

Reduce the pressure with cold water. Place the chicken joints on a serving dish and keep warm. Return the open cooker to the heat and cook the sauce over a high heat, until it has reduced by half. Stir in the cream, reheat (but do not boil) and check the seasoning. Spoon over the chicken pieces and serve with rice.

Devilled Turkey Legs

Score the turkey legs in 3 or 4 places. In a bowl mix together the mustard, chutney, Tabasco, oil, cayenne pepper and parsley. Spread this mixture over the turkey legs.

Place the greased trivet in the base of the cooker and pour in the water. Place the legs on the trivet. Bring to high pressure and cook for 10 minutes.

Reduce the pressure with cold water. Lift out the turkey legs and brown under a hot grill for 2–3 minutes before serving. Serve tomato sauce (see page 124) separately, and a mixed salad.

COOKING TIME 10 minutes
PRESSURE high
SERVES 4

4 turkey legs
2 teaspoons dry mustard
2 tablespoons chutney
few drops Tabasco sauce
6 tablespoons oil
pinch cayenne pepper
2 tablespoons chopped
  parsley
½ pint/3 dl water

Venison Casserole

Cut the venison into cubes and place in a bowl. Pour over the red wine, add the bay leaf, rosemary and peppercorns. Leave in the refrigerator to marinate for at least 1 hour.

Remove the venison from the marinade and pat dry with kitchen paper. Place the bacon and butter in the cooker (with the trivet removed) and heat. Brown the venison cubes on all sides. Add the prepared vegetables and sauté for 3–4 minutes. Pour in the marinade (including the herbs) and stock. Add the sugar, seasoning and bouquet garni, making sure that the cooker is not more than half full. Bring to high pressure and cook for 20 minutes.

Allow the pressure to reduce at room temperature. Discard the bouquet garni and return the open cooker to the heat. Thicken the casserole with the cornflour blended with a little cold water. Check the seasoning and spoon into a serving dish. Serve garnished with chopped parsley.

COOKING TIME 20 minutes,
  plus 1 hour marinating
  time
PRESSURE high
SERVES 4

1½ lb/0.75 kg venison
  haunch
¼ pint/1.5 dl red wine
1 bay leaf
few sprigs fresh
  rosemary
2–3 peppercorns
4 oz/100 g streaky bacon,
  chopped
2 oz/50 g butter
2 onions, chopped
3 carrots, sliced
¾ pint/4.5 dl stock
pinch sugar
salt and pepper
bouquet garni
1 tablespoon cornflour
Garnish
chopped parsley

Duck with Peaches

COOKING TIME 12–15
  minutes per lb (0.5 kg)
PRESSURE high
SERVES 4

2 oz/50 g butter
1 duck
1 oz/25 g sugar
salt and pepper
½ pint/3 dl stock
¼ pint/1.5 dl Madeira
1 8-oz/227-g can peach
  halves
Garnish
watercress

Heat the butter in the open cooker (with the trivet removed) and sauté the duck until browned on all sides, sprinkling with sugar. Remove the duck and place the trivet in the base of the cooker. Replace the duck on the trivet. Sprinkle with salt and pepper and pour in the stock. Bring to high pressure and cook for the calculated time.

Reduce the pressure with cold water. Place the duck on a serving dish and keep warm. Lift out the trivet and skim all the fat from the cooking liquor. Add the Madeira and cook over a high heat until the liquid has reduced by half. Add the drained peaches and allow to heat in the sauce. Check the seasoning, then spoon the peaches and sauce around the duck. Serve garnished with watercress.

Braised Duck

COOKING TIME 12 minutes
PRESSURE high
SERVES 4–6

1 4-lb/1.75-kg duck
2 oz/50 g butter
1 onion, chopped
3 carrots, sliced
2 sticks celery, sliced
bouquet garni
salt and pepper
¼ pint/1.5 dl red wine
¼ pint/1.5 dl stock
grated rind and juice of
  1 orange
1 tablespoon cornflour
Garnish
orange slices
watercress sprigs

Joint the duck. Heat the butter in the open cooker (with the trivet removed) and brown the duck joints. Remove the joints and sauté the prepared vegetables for 3–4 minutes. Replace the joints, add the bouquet garni, seasoning, red wine, stock and orange rind, making sure that the cooker is not more than half full. Bring to high pressure and cook for 12 minutes.

Reduce the pressure with cold water. Arrange the duck and vegetables on a serving dish and keep warm. Return the open cooker to the heat. Remove the bouquet garni and thicken the cooking liquor with the cornflour blended with the orange juice. Check the seasoning and pour over the duck. Serve garnished with orange slices and sprigs of watercress.

Pigeon and Mushroom Casserole

Place the chopped bacon in the cooker (with the trivet removed) and put over a moderate heat until the fat runs. Add the pigeon halves and steak and brown lightly. Add the mushrooms, seasoning, stock and onion, making sure that the cooker is not more than half full. Bring to high pressure and cook for 10 minutes.

Reduce the pressure with cold water. Return the open cooker to the heat and thicken the casserole with the flour blended with a little milk or water. Stir in the lemon juice and redcurrant jelly and simmer for a further 2–3 minutes. Check the seasoning and ladle into a serving dish. Serve garnished with chopped parsley.

COOKING TIME 10 minutes
PRESSURE high
SERVES 4

4 rashers streaky bacon, chopped
2 pigeons, halved
8 oz/225 g skirt steak, cubed
4 oz/100 g button mushrooms
salt and pepper
½ pint/3 dl stock
1 onion, chopped
1 tablespoon flour
squeeze lemon juice
2 tablespoons redcurrant jelly
Garnish
chopped parsley

Pheasant in Madeira

Wipe the pheasant with damp kitchen paper. Make sure it is securely trussed. Heat the butter in the open cooker (with the trivet removed) and sauté the pheasant until browned on all sides. Add the bacon, onion, celery, carrot, seasoning and nutmeg. Pour in the Madeira and stock. Bring to high pressure and cook for 7–10 minutes, depending on the age of the pheasant.

Reduce the pressure with cold water. Lift out the pheasant, place on a serving dish and keep warm. Strain the cooking liquor and place the vegetables and bacon around the pheasant. Boil the cooking liquor until it has reduced by half. Thicken with the cornflour blended with 1 tablespoon water. Check the seasoning and serve with the pheasant.

COOKING TIME 7–10 minutes
PRESSURE high
SERVES 2–4, depending on the size of the bird

1 pheasant, prepared
1 oz/25 g butter
4 rashers streaky bacon, chopped
1 onion, sliced
1 stick celery, chopped
1 carrot, sliced
salt and pepper
pinch nutmeg
¼ pint/1.5 dl Madeira
¼ pint/1.5 dl stock
2 teaspoons cornflour

Sherried kidneys (see page 95)

Vegetables

Vegetables are an essential part of our diet and as well as being served as accompaniments they make excellent dishes in their own right. A wide selection of vegetables is available throughout the year and when bought in season represent good value for money.

Fresh vegetables do need a certain amount of preparation, but by cooking them in a pressure cooker (either in the separators as the accompaniment to the main course, or as a dish on their own) there is an enormous saving both in time and fuel consumption. Another plus factor for using the pressure cooker for vegetables is that by cooking them in the absence of light and air and in steam as opposed to water they retain colour, flavour, texture and nutritive values. Even when cooking a selection of different vegetables simultaneously, there is no danger of the flavours becoming intermingled.

Be selective when purchasing vegetables and reject ones which are limp, shrivelled and looking decidedly antique. Remember that a pressure cooker cannot wave a magic wand over stale vegetables and turn them into fresh ones!

For freezer owners and allotment addicts, the pressure cooker is ideal for blanching vegetables prior to freezing. It makes light work of what can be a rather tiresome job.

When cooking a selection of vegetables simultaneously, if they do not all require the same cooking time, the ones needing the longest cooking must be cut smaller.

With pressure cooking, timing is all-important and if vegetables are allowed longer than the times given you will be disappointed with results. Remember that age, freshness and the size of the vegetables will all affect the cooking time.

When it comes to cooking frozen vegetables, I think it is preferable to cook them in an ordinary pan, as the cooking time will be short, due to the fact that they have been previously blanched.

Fennel and tomato niçoise (see page 88), scalloped potatoes (see page 86) and spicy red cabbage (see page 87)

Rules for pressure cooking fresh vegetables

1 Prepare the vegetables according to kind–see the chart on pages 80 to 83.

2 Pour the necessary amount of liquid into the cooker–either ¼ pint (1.5 dl) or ½ pint (3 dl), but this will depend on your type of cooker, so check with the manufacturer's leaflet.

3 Place the trivet in the base of the cooker. Add the prepared vegetables either in the separators, or they may be placed directly on the trivet. Add a *sprinkling* of salt–beware of adding as much salt as you would if cooking the vegetables in an ordinary pan.

Do not fill the cooker more than two-thirds full of vegetables if you are cooking them on the trivet and not using the separators. The steam must have sufficient room to circulate.

4 Bring to high pressure and cook for the calculated time, see the chart on pages 80 to 83.

5 At the end of the cooking time reduce the pressure with cold water. This should be done immediately to prevent the vegetables becoming overcooked. Reducing the pressure at room temperature would lead to the same results–overcooked, unappetising vegetables.

6 Tip the vegetables from the separators (no draining is necessary) into a serving dish. If they have been cooked on the trivet, remove them with a spoon.

7 Do not waste the cooking liquor in the bottom of the cooker–utilise it in sauces, gravies or in stock, soups or stews.

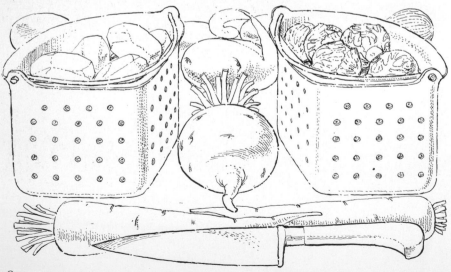

To blanch vegetables for freezing

1 Prepare the vegetables according to kind–see the chart on pages 80 to 83.

2 Pour the necessary amount of liquid into the cooker–either $\frac{1}{4}$ pint (1.5 dl) or $\frac{1}{2}$ pint (3 dl), but this will depend on your type of cooker, so check with the manufacturer's leaflet.

3 Place the trivet in the base of the cooker and bring the water to the boil. Add the prepared vegetables, in the perforated separators for green and small vegetables, or directly on the trivet for others, making sure that the cooker is not more than two-thirds full.

4 Bring to medium pressure and blanch for the calculated time–see the chart on pages 80 to 83.

5 Reduce the pressure *immediately* with cold water, then tip the vegetables into a bowl of cold water with ice cubes added.

6 Drain and then dry on kitchen paper. Pack, seal and label.

Note

With some pressure cookers a blanching basket is available, which makes the blanching process easier and quicker. It avoids having to retrieve the vegetables with a straining spoon after blanching each batch.

If you freeze down vegetables, a blanching basket makes the process quicker and easier. The basket may be purchased as an optional extra with some types of pressure cookers.

The times given vary according to the size of the vegetables and their age.

Vegetable preparation	Cooking time (high pressure)	Blanching time for freezing (medium pressure)	Serving suggestion
Asparagus Wash, trim and tie in bundles each containing 4–6 spears. Place on trivet.	2–4 minutes	Just bring to pressure	With melted butter, hollandaise or mousseline sauce (see page 126).
Broad beans Pod and place in separator.	4–5 minutes	1 minute	With parsley sauce (see page 125).
Beetroot (see note) Cut off tops, leaving 1 inch (2.5 cm) of stem. Peel when cooked.	10 minutes (small) 15–20 minutes (medium) 25–30 minutes (large)	7 minutes (sliced)	Hot with béchamel sauce (see page 125) or soured cream; cold with vinegar.
Broccoli Trim and divide into spears. Place in separator.	3–4 minutes	1 minute	With melted butter and a sprinkling of nutmeg or ground black pepper.
Brussels sprouts Trim and cut a cross in the base of each. Place in separator.	3–4 minutes	1 minute	With cooked chestnuts, melted butter or a sprinkling of grated nutmeg.
Cabbage Trim, discard stalk and shred. Place in separator.	3 minutes	Just bring to pressure	With melted butter, or a few caraway seeds.
Carrots Peel, slice, or cut into sticks. Young ones may be left whole. Place in separator, or on the trivet.	3–4 minutes	2 minutes	With melted butter, black pepper and chopped parsley.

Vegetable preparation	Cooking time (high pressure)	Blanching time for freezing (medium pressure)	Serving suggestion
Cauliflower Trim and divide into sprigs. Place on the trivet.	3–4 minutes 5–8 minutes (whole)	1 minute	With béchamel or cheese sauce (see page 125).
Celery Trim and cut into 2-inch (5-cm) lengths. Place in separator, or on trivet.	3–4 minutes	2 minutes	With béchamel sauce (see page 125).
Celeriac Peel and cube, or cut into 1-inch (2.5-cm) sticks. Cover with cold water until ready to place in separator.	3 minutes	1 minute	With parsley or cheese sauce (see page 125).
Chicory Discard any loose outer leaves. Place whole on trivet, dot with butter and sprinkle with lemon juice.	3–6 minutes	Not suitable for freezing	With béchamel or cheese sauce (see page 125).
Corn-on-the-cob Remove leaves and silks. Place whole on trivet.	3 minutes (small) 5 minutes (large)	2 minutes 3 minutes	With ground black pepper and melted butter.
Courgettes Slice. Place in separator.	3 minutes	Just bring to pressure	With melted butter, black pepper and chopped chives.
Fennel Trim, discard leafy tops and halve. Place on trivet.	3–6 minutes	1 minute	With cheese sauce (see page 125).

Vegetable preparation	Cooking time (high pressure)	Blanching time for freezing (medium pressure)	Serving suggestion
French beans Top, tail and place on trivet.	3 minutes	Just bring to pressure	With melted butter, or cold in a salad.
Globe artichokes Remove outer leaves. Place on trivet.	6 minutes (small) 10 minutes (large)	3 minutes (small) 5 minutes (large)	With melted butter, or French dressing.
Jerusalem artichokes Peel. Place on trivet.	4–5 minutes	Freeze cooked as a purée with lemon juice added. Use for soup.	With melted butter and black pepper.
Kohl-rabi Discard outer leaves, peel and cut into $\frac{1}{4}$-inch (5-mm) slices. Place in separator.	4 minutes		With cheese or hollandaise sauce (see pages 125 and 126).
Leeks Trim and slice. Wash well. Place in separator.	2–3 minutes	1 minute	With béchamel or cheese sauce (see page 125).
Marrow Skin, slice thickly and discard seeds. Place on trivet.	4 minutes	2 minutes	With béchamel or cheese sauce (see page 125).
Onions Peel and slice. Place in separator. Peel, leave whole and place on trivet.	4 minutes 6–8 minutes	Not really worth freezing	With béchamel or cheese sauce (see page 125).
Parsnips Peel and cube. Place in separator or on trivet.	3–4 minutes	1 minute	With butter and black pepper.

Vegetable preparation	Cooking time (high pressure)	Blanching time for freezing (medium pressure)	Serving suggestion
Peas Shell. Place in separator with a sprig of mint.	3–4 minutes	1 minute	With melted butter.
Potatoes (new) Scrape and leave whole. Place in separator or on trivet.	4–5 minutes	2 minutes	With melted butter and chopped parsley or chives.
Potatoes (old) Peel and quarter. Place in separator or on trivet.	3–4 minutes	Not really worth freezing	Creamed with butter and hot milk; with a knob of butter and chopped parsley.
Runner beans String and slice.	4 minutes	To pressure only	With a knob of butter.
Swedes Peel and cube. Place in separator.	4 minutes	1 minute	Mashed with butter and seasoned with black pepper.
Turnips Peel and slice. Place in separator.	3–4 minutes	2 minutes	Mashed with butter.
Young, whole, place on trivet or in separator.	3–4 minutes	2 minutes	With melted butter and black pepper.

Note
When pressure cooking beetroots, as the cooking time is longer, a greater amount of water must be put in the cooker before it is brought to pressure.

For small beetroots allow 1 pint (6 dl) water.
For medium beetroots allow 1½ pints (9 dl) water.
For large beetroots allow 2 pints (generous 1 litre) water.

Vegetables which are not included in the chart, aubergines, mushrooms, spinach, peppers, do not ideally lend themselves to pressure cooking. Mushrooms, especially the large black ones, are better grilled with a knob of butter or fried in a mixture of oil and butter. Spinach cooks very quickly in an ordinary pan in a minute amount of water. Whole peppers can be stuffed and pressure cooked (see page 89), or added to casseroles, stews and vegetable dishes. Aubergines need to be salted and drained, prior to cooking in a mixture of butter and oil; or egg and crumbed and deep fried.

The dried vegetables (butter beans, haricot beans, lentils, whole and split peas) are worth cooking under pressure, as there is a time saving and the need for overnight soaking is eliminated; they need to soak for 1 hour prior to cooking.

Rules for pressure cooking dried vegetables

1 Strain (and keep) the soaking water from the vegetables. Make it up to 2 pints (generous 1 litre) for every 1 lb (450 g) of vegetables. Pour the measured amount of water into the cooker with the trivet removed.

2 Bring to the boil and add the vegetables, making sure that the cooker is not more than half full. Season with salt and pepper and add a bouquet garni if liked. Bring back to the boil and, with a slotted draining spoon, remove the scum that rises.

3 Lower the heat, secure the lid, and weight and bring to high pressure. (It is necessary to bring to pressure with the source of heat turned low, so that the vegetables and water do not rise up during the cooking.)

4 Cook for the calculated time (see the table below) and allow the pressure to reduce at room temperature.

Vegetable	Cooking time
Butter beans	20 minutes
Haricot beans (large)	30 minutes
Haricot beans (small)	20 minutes
Lentils	15 minutes
Split peas	15 minutes
Whole peas	20 minutes

Savoury Stuffed Onions

COOKING TIME 8 minutes
PRESSURE high
SERVE 4

4 large onions
½ pint/3 dl water
1 oz/25 g butter
4 oz/100 g bacon, chopped
salt and pepper
pinch dry mustard
2 oz/50 g fresh
  breadcrumbs
1 egg
2 tablespoons cream
2 oz/50 g cheese, grated

Peel the onions, but leave whole. Put the water and trivet in the bottom of the cooker and place the onions on the trivet. Bring to high pressure and cook for 8 minutes.

Meanwhile, heat the butter in a pan and add the chopped bacon. Cook for 2–3 minutes, then stir in the seasonings and breadcrumbs and heat through. Lightly beat the egg and cream together and mix into the bacon mixture. Leave on a low heat.

Reduce the pressure with cold water. Take out the onions, slice off the tops and remove the centres, leaving a shell ½–1 inch (1–2.5 cm) thick. Chop the centres and tops and mix into the filling. Place the onion shells in the grill pan (with the rack removed) and spoon in the filling. Sprinkle the tops with grated cheese and brown under a moderate grill.

If liked, serve with tomato sauce (see page 124).

Broad Beans with Cream and Almonds

COOKING TIME 4–5 minutes
PRESSURE high
SERVES 4

½ pint/3 dl water
1 lb/0.5 kg shelled broad
  beans
1 oz/25 g butter
¼ pint/1.5 dl single cream
salt and pepper
2 tablespoons chopped
  parsley
2 oz/50 g flaked almonds

Pour the water in the bottom of the cooker. Put in the trivet and cover with the beans. Bring to high pressure and cook for 4–5 minutes.

Reduce the pressure with cold water. Heat the butter in a pan and add the beans; turn until coated with the butter. Add the cream and seasoning and heat, but do not allow the cream to boil. Stir in the chopped parsley and spoon into a serving dish. Sprinkle over the almonds.

Variation

Whole French beans may be cooked in the same way—allow 3 minutes cooking time at high pressure. In place of the almonds, sprinkle with chopped spring onions.

85

Lettuce-Braised French Beans

Trim the beans and if young leave whole, otherwise cut into 2-inch (5-cm) pieces. Peel the onions and leave whole. Wash and drain the lettuce.

Heat the butter in the open cooker (with the trivet removed) and arrange the lettuce leaves in a layer in the bottom of the cooker. Add the beans, onions, water, sugar, seasoning and bouquet garni. Bring to high pressure and cook for 3 minutes.

Reduce the pressure with cold water. Spoon the beans and onions into a dish and serve, adding a little of the cooking liquid.

Note

So as not to waste any of the good ingredients I liquidise the lettuce and cooking liquid. When chilled and mixed with single cream it makes a delicious cold soup. Serve with a sprinkling of chopped chives.

COOKING TIME 3 minutes
PRESSURE high
SERVES 4

1½ lb/0.75 kg French beans
8 oz/225 g small onions
1 lettuce
2 oz/50 g butter
¼ pint/1.5 dl water
pinch sugar
salt and pepper
bouquet garni

Scalloped Potatoes

Peel and slice the potatoes and dry on kitchen paper. Melt the butter in the open cooker (with the trivet removed), add the garlic, milk and water and bring to the boil. Layer in the potato slices, sprinkling with the seasonings. Bring to high pressure and cook for 5 minutes.

Reduce the pressure with cold water, lift out the potatoes and place in an ovenproof dish. Spoon over some of the cooking liquid. Sprinkle the surface with the cheeses and brown under a hot grill. Serve garnished with chopped chives or parsley sprig.

COOKING TIME 5 minutes
PRESSURE high
SERVES 4

1½ lb/0.75 kg potatoes
2 oz/50 g butter
1 clove garlic, crushed
¼ pint/1.5 dl milk
¼ pint/1.5 dl water
salt and pepper
little grated nutmeg
2 oz/50 g Gruyère cheese, grated
1 tablespoon grated Parmesan cheese
Garnish
chopped chives or parsley sprig
Illustrated on page 76

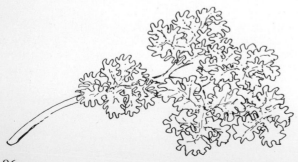

Spicy Red Cabbage

COOKING TIME 5 minutes
PRESSURE high
SERVES 4

4 rashers streaky bacon,
  chopped
1 onion, chopped
1 small red cabbage
2 cooking apples
3 tablespoons wine
  vinegar
2 tablespoons brown sugar
6 tablespoons water
salt and pepper
1–2 cloves
little grated nutmeg
Illustrated on page 76

Place the chopped bacon in the open cooker (with the trivet removed). Cook over a moderate heat until the fat runs, then add the onion and sauté for 2–3 minutes.

Cut the cabbage into quarters, discard the stalk, and shred finely. Peel, core and cube the apples. Add the cabbage, apples, vinegar, sugar, water, salt, pepper, cloves and nutmeg. Bring to high pressure and cook for 5 minutes.

Allow the pressure to reduce at room temperature. Check the seasoning, then spoon into a warm serving dish.

This is excellent served with pork or duck.

Cauliflower Italian Style

COOKING TIME 3–4 minutes
PRESSURE high
SERVES 4

1 cauliflower
½ pint/3 dl water
2 oz/50 g butter, melted
4 oz/100 g Gruyère or
  Cheddar cheese, grated
salt and pepper
pinch oregano

Trim the cauliflower and divide into sprigs. Pour the water into the cooker and place the trivet in the bottom. Put the cauliflower on the trivet and season lightly with salt. Bring to high pressure and cook for 3–4 minutes.

Reduce the pressure with cold water. Transfer the cauliflower to a greased ovenproof dish. Pour over the melted butter, sprinkle with grated cheese, seasoning and oregano and brown under a hot grill for 2–3 minutes.

Celery with Herbs

Wash the celery and cut the sticks into 2-inch (5-cm) lengths. Pour the liquid into the cooker and place the trivet in the bottom. Place the celery on the trivet and sprinkle over the herbs and seasoning. Bring to high pressure and cook for 3–4 minutes.

Reduce the pressure with cold water. Place the celery in a warm serving dish and spoon over the cooking liquid. Serve sprinkled with paprika.

COOKING TIME 3–4 minutes
PRESSURE high
SERVES 4

1 head celery
½ pint/3 dl water, stock or dry white wine
1 teaspoon chopped tarragon
1–2 tablespoons chopped parsley
salt and pepper

Fennel and Tomato Niçoise

Heat the oil in the open cooker (with the trivet removed) and sauté the onion and garlic for 3–4 minutes. Trim and cut the fennel into quarters. Add to the cooker together with the tomatoes, water, thyme, seasoning, sugar and olives, making sure that the cooker is not more than half full. Bring to high pressure and cook for 5 minutes.

Reduce the pressure with cold water. Check the seasoning and spoon into a serving dish.

COOKING TIME 5 minutes
PRESSURE high
SERVES 4

2 tablespoons oil
1 onion, chopped
1 clove garlic, crushed
4 bulbs fennel
1 15-oz/425-g can tomatoes
¼ pint/1.5 dl water
pinch thyme
salt and pepper
pinch sugar
6–8 black olives, stoned
Illustrated on page 76

Ways to serve asparagus

Cook the asparagus according to the chart on page 80 and serve in any of the following ways:
Asparagus with hollandaise sauce
Arrange the cooked asparagus on a warm serving dish and spoon over hollandaise sauce (see page 126).
Asparagus with cheese
Dip each cooked asparagus spear in melted butter, then coat with grated cheese. Arrange on a warm serving dish, pour over a little more melted butter and sprinkle with salt and pepper.

Asparagus au gratin
Arrange the cooked asparagus in an ovenproof dish. Pour over ½ pint (3 dl) béchamel sauce (see page 125), sprinkle with fresh breadcrumbs and grated cheese and brown under a heated grill.
Asparagus with ham
Place two cooked and cooled asparagus spears on a piece of cooked ham. Form into a roll and serve, cold, with French dressing mixed with chopped parsley and chopped hard-boiled egg.

Leeks à la Grecque

COOKING TIME 3 minutes
PRESSURE high
SERVES 4

2 lb/1 kg leeks
2 oz/50 g butter
¼ pint/1.5 dl stock
¼ pint/1.5 dl dry white wine
1 tablespoon tomato purée
1 bay leaf
salt and pepper
paprika pepper

Trim the leeks, discarding most of the green tops. Slice and wash well.

Heat the butter in the open cooker (with the trivet removed) and sauté the leeks for 1–2 minutes. Add the stock, wine, tomato purée, bay leaf and seasoning. Bring to high pressure and cook for 3 minutes.

Reduce the pressure with cold water. Transfer the leeks, discarding the bay leaf, to a serving dish and keep warm. Return the open cooker to the heat and boil the cooking liquor until it has reduced by half. Pour over the leeks and serve garnished with a sprinkling of paprika.

Tuna-Stuffed Peppers

COOKING TIME 5 minutes
PRESSURE high
SERVES 4

1 7-oz/198-g can tuna fish
2 tablespoons cooked long-grain rice
1 onion, grated
salt and pepper
1 tablespoon chopped parsley
4 even-sized green peppers
½ pint/3 dl water
2 oz/50 g cheese, grated

Drain and flake the tuna and mix with the rice, onion, seasoning and parsley.

Cut off the stem end of each pepper and scoop out the seeds. Divide the filling between the prepared peppers.

Pour the water into the cooker and place the trivet in the bottom. Stand the peppers on the trivet. Bring to high pressure and cook for 5 minutes.

Reduce the pressure with cold water. Lift the peppers onto an ovenproof dish, sprinkle the tops with grated cheese and brown under a moderate grill. If liked serve with tomato sauce (see page 124).

Spinach and Cheese Pudding

Place the milk, butter and bay leaf in a pan. Heat slowly to just below boiling, then remove from the heat. Discard the bay leaf and pour over the breadcrumbs. Leave to stand for 30 minutes.

Mix in the spinach, egg yolks, seasonings and cheese. Whisk the egg whites until stiff then fold into the spinach mixture. Place the mixture in a greased 2-pint (generous 1-litre) ovenproof bowl and cover with a double layer of greased greaseproof paper secured with string.

Pour the boiling water into the cooker and place the trivet in the bottom. Stand the bowl on the trivet. Bring to high pressure and cook for 20 minutes.

Allow the pressure to reduce at room temperature. Lift out the pudding, take off the papers and serve at once. A green or winter salad is a good accompaniment to this spinach pudding.

COOKING TIME 20 minutes
PRESSURE high
SERVES 4

$\frac{1}{4}$ pint/1.5 dl milk
1 oz/25 g butter
1 bay leaf
2 oz/50 g fresh bread-
  crumbs
1 8-oz/227-g packet
  frozen spinach, thawed
3 eggs, separated
salt and pepper
little grated nutmeg
2 oz/50 g cheese, grated
1 pint/6 dl boiling water

Haricot Beans with Tomatoes

Place the beans in a bowl, cover with boiling water and leave to soak for 1 hour.

Drain off and measure the bean soaking liquid. Make up to 1$\frac{3}{4}$ pints (1 litre) with cold water and pour into the cooker (with the trivet removed). Bring to the boil in the open cooker and add the beans, making sure that the cooker is not more than half full. Remove the scum that rises to the surface and add the onion and bouquet garni. Lower the heat, bring to high pressure and cook for 20 minutes.

Allow the pressure to reduce at room temperature. Meanwhile, skin and slice the tomatoes. Heat the butter in a pan and sauté the tomatoes for 3–4 minutes. Stir in the beans, salt, pepper and cream. Allow the cream to heat through, then spoon into a dish and serve garnished with a sprinkling of paprika.

COOKING TIME 20 minutes,
  plus 1 hour for soaking
PRESSURE high
SERVES 4

1 lb/450 g small haricot
  beans
1 onion, sliced
bouquet garni
4 large tomatoes
2 oz/50 g butter
salt and pepper
$\frac{1}{4}$ pint/1.5 dl single cream
Garnish
paprika pepper

All-in-One Meals

The recipes in this section are ideal for bachelor cooks who may have only a single burner on which to cook, for self-catering holidaymakers on a caravanning, camping or boating holiday and for those times when you need to provide a meal quickly. An added bonus is of course the fact that the washing up is kept to a minimum.

Many of the other main course recipes in the book may also become all-in-one meals by cooking your chosen vegetables simultaneously.

Savoury Risotto

COOKING TIME 8 minutes
PRESSURE high
SERVES 4

2 oz/50 g butter
1 onion, chopped
1 stick celery, chopped
2 oz/50 g mushrooms, sliced
1 pepper, seeded and chopped
8 oz/225 g long-grain rice
1 small can luncheon meat, cubed
1 pint/6 dl stock or water
salt and pepper
1 bay leaf
2 oz/50 g cheese, grated
1–2 teaspoons chopped parsley

Heat the butter in the open cooker (with the trivet removed) and sauté the prepared vegetables for 2–3 minutes. Stir in the rice and luncheon meat. Add the stock, seasoning and bay leaf, making sure that the cooker is not more than half full. Over a moderate heat, bring to high pressure and cook for 8 minutes.

Allow the pressure to reduce at room temperature. Return the open cooker to a low heat and with a fork, fluff up the rice until the grains are separate. Discard the bay leaf. Check the seasoning and serve sprinkled with grated cheese and chopped parsley.

Gammon Steaks in Cider

Trim the rinds from the gammon steaks and snip the fat at intervals. Heat the oil in the open cooker (with the trivet removed) and brown the gammon steaks on each side. Remove and brown the drained pineapple rings on each side. Remove. Wipe out the cooker with kitchen paper. Place the gammon steaks with a ring of pineapple on each in the base of the cooker, overlapping them slightly. Sprinkle with rosemary and pepper. Pour in the cider. Place in the trivet and put the prepared potatoes (cut into large cubes, or use small, whole new ones) on one half of the trivet. Place the prepared beans in the perforated separator and place on the trivet. Sprinkle the vegetables lightly with salt.

Bring to high pressure and cook for 5 minutes. Allow the pressure to reduce at room temperature. Transfer the vegetables to serving dishes; garnish the potatoes with chopped parsley. Arrange the gammon and pineapple on a serving plate and spoon over the cooking liquor. Serve garnished with watercress.

COOKING TIME 5 minutes
PRESSURE high
SERVES 4

4 gammon steaks
1 tablespoon oil
1 small can pineapple rings
few sprigs fresh or pinch
   dried rosemary
salt and pepper
½ pint/3 dl dry cider
1 lb/0.5 kg potatoes
1 lb/0.5 kg French beans
Garnish
chopped parsley
sprigs watercress
Illustrated opposite

Hunter's Stew

Trim the pork and cut into cubes. Toss lightly in a little flour seasoned with salt and pepper. Heat the oil in the open cooker (with the trivet removed) and sauté the pieces of meat until browned on all sides. Add the prepared onion and carrots and sauté for a further 1–2 minutes. Stir in the tomatoes, stock, curry paste, chutney and brown sugar, making sure that the cooker is not more than half full. Bring to high pressure and cook for 25 minutes.

Allow the pressure to reduce at room temperature. Return the open cooker to the heat and add the frozen peas. Cook for 5 minutes in the open cooker. Check the seasoning and serve with crusty French bread and a salad.

COOKING TIME 25 minutes
PRESSURE high
SERVES 4

1 lb/0.5 kg pork leg or
   fillet
flour
salt and pepper
1 tablespoon oil
1 large onion, chopped
4 carrots, sliced
1 16-oz/450-g can
   tomatoes
½ pint/3 dl stock or water
½ teaspoon curry paste
1 tablespoon chutney
1 tablespoon brown sugar
1 8-oz/225-g packet frozen
   peas

Gammon steaks in cider (see above)

Lamb Casserole

COOKING TIME 15 minutes
PRESSURE high
SERVES 4

4 lamb chops
salt and pepper
pinch mixed herbs
½ pint/3 dl stock or water
2 onions, sliced
4 small carrots
1 lb/0.5 kg potatoes, sliced
Garnish
chopped parsley

Remove the excess fat from the chops and season the chops on each side with salt, pepper and the mixed herbs. Place the chops in the bottom of the cooker (with the trivet removed). Pour in the stock or water. Arrange the prepared vegetables on top of the meat. Bring to high pressure and cook for 15 minutes.

Allow the pressure to reduce at room temperature. Check the seasoning and serve garnished with chopped parsley.

Sherried Kidneys

Skin, slice and remove the cores from the kidneys. Heat the butter in the open cooker (with the trivet removed) and sauté the onion for 5 minutes. Add the prepared kidneys and cook for 2 minutes until firm and sealed; do not overcook them at this stage. Add the tomato purée, bay leaf, sherry, stock, seasoning and mustard, making sure that the cooker is not more than half full. Place the trivet on top of the kidneys. Place the rice in the solid separator with the water or stock and cover with a piece of foil. Bring to high pressure and cook for 5 minutes.

Allow the pressure to reduce at room temperature. Fluff up the rice with a fork. Discard the bay leaf from the kidneys, return the open cooker to the heat and thicken the liquid with the blended flour. Check the seasoning, stir in the chopped parsley and serve with the rice. Garnish with a sprig of parsley.

COOKING TIME 5 minutes
PRESSURE high
SERVES 4

12 lambs' kidneys
1 oz/25 g butter
1 onion, chopped
1 tablespoon tomato
  purée
1 bay leaf
¼ pint/1.5 dl dry sherry
¼ pint/1.5 dl stock or water
salt and pepper
pinch dry mustard
6 oz/175 g long-grain rice
scant ½ pint/2.5 dl lightly
  salted water or stock
1 oz/25 g flour
2 tablespoons chopped
  parsley
Illustrated on page 75

Candied rice pudding and rice condé (see page 105)

Beef and Bean Savoury

Heat the oil in the open cooker (with the trivet removed) and sauté the minced beef until browned on all sides. Stir in the onions, tomatoes, chilli powder, seasoning and stock, making sure that the cooker is not more than half full. Bring to high pressure and cook for 15 minutes.

Allow the pressure to reduce at room temperature. Return the open cooker to the heat and stir in the baked beans with sausages. Simmer for 2–3 minutes. Check the seasoning and garnish with parsley. Serve with crusty rolls or French bread, and a salad.

All-in-one meals may be cooked in a pressure cooker. These are ideal to serve when you are in a hurry and the washing up is kept to a minimum.

COOKING TIME 15 minutes
PRESSURE high
SERVES 4

2 tablespoons oil
1 lb/0.5 kg minced beef
2 onions, sliced
1 8-oz/225-g can tomatoes
2–3 teaspoons chilli powder
salt and pepper
¼ pint/1.5 dl stock or water
1 7¾-oz/220-g can baked
  beans with sausages

Illustrated on page 17

Traditional Beef Curry

COOKING TIME 20 minutes
PRESSURE high
SERVES 4

¼ pint/1.5 dl oil
1 lb/0.5 kg onions, sliced
3–4 tablespoons curry
  powder
2–3 tablespoons malt
  vinegar
1½ lb/0.75 kg braising
  steak, cubed
1 12-oz/350-g can tomatoes
¼ pint/1.5 dl stock
2 bay leaves
salt and pepper
Rice
8 oz/225 g long-grain rice
1 teaspoon turmeric
3 cloves
1 bay leaf
¾ pint/4.5 dl lightly salted
  boiling water
Side dishes
½ cucumber
1 small carton natural
  yogurt
4 tomatoes
1 onion
2–3 tablespoons malt
  vinegar
chilli powder (optional)
Illustrated on page 58

This is a traditional recipe for beef curry given to me by a friend who was brought up in India. I have adapted it for pressure cooking, but the end result is still authentic. The rice can also be cooked under pressure in an ovenproof bowl. Cooking a curry this way is almost as quick as going to the take away restaurant!

Heat the oil in the open cooker and sauté the prepared onions for 10 minutes. This should be done over a low heat until the onions have softened and are just turning yellow and transparent. Blend the curry powder to a smooth paste with the vinegar. Stir into the onions and cook for a further 2–3 minutes. Add the cubes of meat and stir into the onion and curry mixture until the meat cubes become coated with the blended curry. Stir in the tomatoes, stock, bay leaves and seasoning. Bring to high pressure and cook for 15 minutes.

Allow the pressure to reduce with cold water. Place the rice in an ovenproof bowl, mix in the turmeric and add the cloves and bay leaf. Pour in the water and cover with a piece of foil.

Remove the lid from the cooker, place the trivet over the curry and the ovenproof bowl on the trivet. Re-fit the lid, bring back to high pressure and cook for 5 minutes. Allow the pressure to reduce at room temperature.

Meanwhile, prepare the curry accompaniments. Cube the cucumber and mix with the yogurt. Place in a small serving dish. Quarter or slice the tomatoes and slice the onion. Mix together and place in a second small serving dish. Pour over the vinegar and if liked sprinkle with chilli powder—not too much as it is very hot.

To serve the curry, remove the lid from the cooker. Lift out the bowl and fluff up the rice with a fork. Discard the cloves and bay leaf and arrange around the edge of a warm serving dish. Check the seasoning of the curry, then spoon into the centre of the dish. Serve with the side dishes and mango chutney, if liked.

Desserts

A variety of desserts may be made in the pressure cooker. Steamed puddings are particularly suitable and cook very quickly compared with the traditional steaming method, and your kitchen doesn't become like a Turkish bath in the process!

Fresh fruits may be cooked under pressure, but I wouldn't recommend you cook the soft fruits this way as their normal cooking times are so short. Dried fruits and the packets of mixed dried fruits are excellent pressure cooked; egg custards and milk puddings are also suitable.

Rules for pressure cooking steamed puddings
1 Use an ovenproof basin for the pudding mixture— made of ovenproof glass or china; enamel; metal. When using either ovenproof glass or china allow an additional 5 minutes cooking time. This is because they are not such good conductors of heat as enamel and metal.
2 Do not fill the greased basin more than two-thirds full. Sufficient room must be allowed for the pudding to rise during cooking.

3 Cover the pudding with foil or a double layer of greased greaseproof paper and tie it securely under the rim of the basin. It is advisable to put a pleat in the paper should the pudding rise to above the top of the basin.

4 The trivet is used to stand the basin on.

5 The amount of water required depends on the length of the cooking time, but is never less than 2 pints (generous 1 litre). *Boiling* water is put into the cooker–not cold water brought to the boil in the open cooker as some of the measured amount would be lost due to evaporation.

6 If you live in a hard water area add a little lemon juice or vinegar to the water to prevent the inside of the cooker becoming discoloured. Hard water discolours aluminium cookers, but if yours has a non-stick lining it shouldn't be badly affected.

7 Steamed puddings are pre-steamed before being brought to pressure to allow the mixture to rise. This is done to give a light texture to the cooked pudding. Pre-steaming is done over a low heat with the lid on the cooker, but without the weight. After pre-steaming the cooker is brought to low pressure in the normal way.

8 At the end of the cooking time allow the pressure to reduce at room temperature.

When cooking steamed puddings in the pressure cooker, cover the basin with a double layer of greased greaseproof paper, or foil, and secure it under the rim of the basin.

Rules for pressure cooking fresh fruits
1 Place the trivet and ½ pint (3 dl) water in the bottom of the cooker.
2 Place the prepared fruit in an ovenproof container. Sprinkle with castor sugar, or make a medium strength sugar syrup with 3–4 tablespoons castor sugar and ¼ pint (1.5 dl) water. Cover the ovenproof container with foil or a double layer of greaseproof paper.
3 Stand the container on the trivet, bring to pressure and cook for the required time, see the chart below.

Note
When bulk cooking fruits (for puréeing) such as apples, gooseberries and rhubarb they may be placed directly in the cooker with a minimum of ½ pint (3 dl) liquid (water, syrup or juice), ensuring that the cooker is not more than half full, and brought to medium pressure over a moderate heat. Allow the pressure to reduce at room temperature.

Fruit preparation	Cooking time and pressure	Use
Apples Peel, core and slice. Pack in ovenproof basin and sprinkle with sugar (or add a sugar syrup). Add a grating of nutmeg, or 1–2 cloves, if liked. Cover.	1 minute at medium pressure. Allow pressure to reduce at room temperature.	In tarts, flans, charlottes and crumbles. As an accompaniment to roast pork. *To freeze* Mash or purée in the liquidiser. Cool and pack in polythene containers.
Apricots Halve and stone. Pack in ovenproof basin and sprinkle with sugar (or add a sugar syrup). Cover.	Just bring to high pressure. Reduce pressure immediately with cold water.	In tarts, flans, charlottes and crumbles. As a purée in soufflés, mousses and fools, or over ice cream. *To freeze* Mash or purée in the liquidiser. Cool and pack in polythene containers.
Cherries Remove stalks and stones (or remove stones when cooked). Pack in ovenproof basin and sprinkle with sugar (or add a sugar syrup). Cover.	Just bring to high pressure. Reduce pressure immediately with cold water.	In tarts, cooked pastry or sponge flan cases.

Fruit preparation	Cooking time and pressure	Use
Damsons, greengages Halve and stone. Or cook whole, pricking each one with a fork. Remove stones when cooked. Pack in ovenproof basin and sprinkle with sugar (or add a sugar syrup). Cover.	Just bring to high pressure. Reduce pressure immediately with cold water.	In tarts, cooked pastry or sponge flan cases.
Peaches Remove skins by plunging into boiling water for 1–2 minutes. Halve and stone. Pack in ovenproof basin and sprinkle with sugar (or add a sugar syrup). Cover.	3–5 minutes (depending on size) at high pressure. Reduce pressure with cold water.	In cooked pastry or sponge flan cases. With jam sauce (or raspberry purée) and ice cream, making peach melba.
Pears Peel, halve and core. Place directly on trivet. Add sugar or a sugar syrup.	3–5 minutes (depending on size) at high pressure. Hard stewing pears need 8–10 minutes. Reduce pressure with cold water.	In cooked pastry or sponge flan cases. With chocolate sauce and ice cream.
Plums As for damsons.	Just bring to medium pressure. Reduce pressure immediately with cold water.	As for damsons.
Rhubarb Cut into 1-inch (2.5-cm) lengths. Pack in ovenproof basin and sprinkle with sugar and cinnamon. Cover.	Just bring to medium pressure. Allow pressure to reduce at room temperature.	In tarts, flans or crumbles.

Dried fruits

1 Place the fruit in a basin and cover with boiling water allowing 1 pint (6 dl) water to 1 lb (450 g) fruit. Cover with a plate and leave to soak for 10 minutes.

2 Place the fruit, plus soaking water, in the cooker (with the trivet removed), making sure that the cooker is not more than half full. Add 2–3 tablespoons castor sugar, brown sugar or clear honey and if liked the additions listed in the chart below.

3 Bring to high pressure and cook for the required time– see the table below.

4 Allow the pressure to reduce at room temperature.

Fruit	Add	Cooking time at high pressure
Apples	1–2 cloves	6 minutes
Apricots	1 tablespoon fresh orange juice	3 minutes
Figs	2 teaspoons lemon juice	10 minutes
Peaches	1 tablespoon fresh orange juice	5 minutes
Pears	1–2 cloves	10 minutes
Prunes	grated lemon rind	10 minutes
Mixed fruits	grated lemon rind	10 minutes

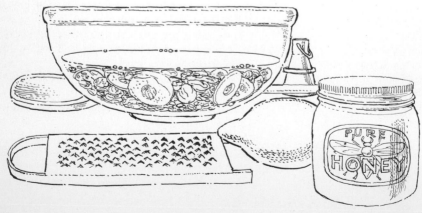

Chancellor's Pudding

COOKING TIME 20 minutes
PRESSURE high
SERVES 6

2 oz/50 g glacé cherries,
  halved
3 tablespoons sherry
3 tablespoons lemon juice
32 sponge finger biscuits
1 oz/25 g angelica, chopped
2 oz/50 g raisins
½ pint/3 dl milk
½ pint/3 dl single cream
4 eggs
4 oz/100 g castor sugar
½ pint/3 dl water

Butter a 2-pint (1.25-litre) pudding basin.

Arrange the halved cherries in the bottom of the basin with the rounded sides down. Mix together the sherry and lemon juice, dip in the sponge fingers and use some to line the sides of the basin so that they fit tightly together. Place the rest of the biscuits, and angelica and raisins on top of the cherries.

Heat the milk and cream to blood heat and pour over the lightly beaten eggs and sugar. Carefully pour into the basin. Cover with foil or a double layer of greased greaseproof paper and tie under the rim.

Pour the water into the cooker, place the trivet in the bottom and put in the pudding. Bring to high pressure and cook for 20 minutes.

Allow the pressure to reduce at room temperature. Lift out the pudding, take off the paper and serve from the basin.

Bread and Butter Pudding

COOKING TIME 6 minutes
PRESSURE high
SERVES 4

6 slices white bread,
  buttered
2 oz/50 g castor sugar
2 oz/50 g currants
2 oz/50 g sultanas
pinch cinnamon
¼ pint/1.5 dl milk
¼ pint/1.5 dl single cream
3 eggs, lightly beaten
½ pint/3 dl water
1 tablespoon demerara
  sugar

Butter an ovenproof dish that can be accommodated in your cooker.

Remove the crusts from the bread and cut each slice into quarters. Arrange the bread, sugar, currants and sultanas in layers in the dish, sprinkling with cinnamon. Heat the milk and cream to blood heat and pour over the lightly beaten eggs. Strain over the bread mixture. Cover the basin with foil or a double layer of greased greaseproof paper and tie under the rim.

Pour the water into the cooker, place the trivet in the bottom and put in the pudding. Bring to high pressure and cook for 6 minutes.

Allow the pressure to reduce at room temperature. Lift out the pudding, take off the paper, sprinkle the surface with demerara sugar and brown lightly under a moderate grill.

Apple and Date Charlotte

Butter an ovenproof dish that can be accommodated in your cooker.

Remove the crusts from the bread and cut the slices to a suitable shape for lining the dish. Melt the butter and dip each piece of bread in melted butter, then in the demerara sugar. Use to line the base and sides of the dish, saving a few pieces for the top.

Peel, core and slice the apples. Layer in the bread-lined dish with the dates and any remaining sugar. Add the clove and remaining bread slices for the top. Cover the dish with foil or a double layer of greased greaseproof paper and tie under the rim.

Pour the water into the cooker, place the trivet in the bottom and put in the charlotte. Bring to high pressure and cook for 12 minutes.

Allow the pressure to reduce at room temperature. Lift out the charlotte, take off the paper and serve from the dish.

COOKING TIME 12 minutes
PRESSURE high
SERVES 4

10 slices white bread
4 oz/100 g butter
4 oz/100 g demerara sugar
1 lb/0.5 kg cooking apples
2 oz/50 g dates, chopped
1 clove
½ pint/3 dl water

Marmalade Pudding

Sieve the flour into a mixing bowl. Stir in the suet and sugar. Mix in half the marmalade, the lightly beaten egg and milk to give a soft mixture. Place the rest of the marmalade in the base of a well-greased 1½-pint (1-litre) pudding basin. Cover with the mixture and smooth the surface. Cover with foil or a double layer of greased greaseproof paper and tie securely under the rim.

Place the trivet in the bottom of the cooker and pour in the boiling water. Stand the pudding on the trivet. Pre-steam (see page 99) for 25 minutes. Bring to low pressure and cook for 25 minutes.

Allow the pressure to reduce at room temperature. Take out the pudding, remove the papers and turn onto a serving dish.

To make the sauce (this can be done while the pressure is reducing), place ¼ pint (1.5 dl) water, orange rind and marmalade in a pan. Bring to the boil, stirring. Thicken with the cornflour blended with the orange juice. Serve separately, or poured over the marmalade pudding.

COOKING TIME 25 minutes
  pre-steaming, 25 minutes
PRESSURE low
SERVES 4

4 oz/100 g self-raising
  flour
2 oz/50 g shredded suet
2 oz/50 g soft brown sugar
3–4 tablespoons thick-cut
  marmalade
1 large egg, lightly beaten
1 tablespoon milk
2 pints/generous 1 litre
  boiling water
Orange sauce
grated rind and juice of
  1 orange
2 tablespoons marmalade
2 teaspoons cornflour

Date-Stuffed Apples

COOKING TIME 4 minutes
PRESSURE high
SERVES 4

4 medium-sized cooking
  apples
4 oz/100 g dates, chopped
4 teaspoons soft brown sugar
grated rind and juice of
  1 orange
½ pint/3 dl water

Wash and core the apples. Score the skin around the widest part of each apple to prevent them bursting. Mix together the dates, sugar, orange rind and juice. Fill the apples with the date mixture.

Pour the water into the cooker and place the trivet in the bottom. Stand the apples on the trivet, bring to high pressure and cook for 4 minutes.

Allow the pressure to reduce at room temperature. Place the apples on a dish and serve with cream.

Rice Pudding

COOKING TIME 12 minutes
PRESSURE high
SERVES 4

½ oz/15 g butter
¾ pint/4.5 dl milk
¼ pint/1.5 dl evaporated
  milk
2 oz/50 g round-grain rice
2 oz/50 g castor sugar
1 small piece cinnamon
  stick
grated rind of 1 lemon

Place the butter in the bottom of the cooker (with the trivet removed) and melt over a moderate heat. Add the milk and evaporated milk and bring to the boil. Add the rice, sugar and cinnamon stick, making sure that the cooker is not more than half full, and bring back to the boil. Adjust the heat so that the milk is simmering. Bring to high pressure on a *low* heat (this is to prevent the pudding rising in the cooker and blocking the air vent) and cook for 12 minutes.

Allow the pressure to reduce at room temperature, then remove the cinnamon stick. Stir in the grated lemon rind and transfer the pudding to a serving dish.

When cooking rice pudding in a pressure cooker which operates at 7½ lb pressure, allow 20 minutes cooking time.

Variations *(Illustrated on page 94)*
Candied rice pudding Spoon the cooked rice pudding into an ovenproof dish. Sprinkle the surface thickly with soft brown sugar and place under a hot grill to caramelise the sugar. Decorate with lemon slices and fresh fruit.
Rice condé This can be made with any cold left-over rice, or allow the rice pudding to cool. Spoon cold rice pudding into individual dishes or one serving dish and mix with drained canned fruit, cooked fresh fruit or fresh or canned fruit salad. Decorate with fruit.

Golden Apricot Pudding

Drain the apricot halves and reserve 3 tablespoons of the juice for the sauce. Place the drained apricots in the base of a greased 1½-pint (1-litre) ovenproof dish or bowl that can be accommodated in your cooker.

To make the topping, cream the sugar and butter together until light and fluffy. Gently mix in the sieved flour and milk. Whisk the egg whites until stiff, then fold into the mixture. Spoon on top of the apricots, filling the dish two-thirds full. Cover with foil or a double layer of greased greaseproof paper and tie.

Place the trivet in the bottom of the cooker and pour in the boiling water. Stand the pudding on the trivet. Pre-steam (see page 99) for 15 minutes. Bring to low pressure and cook for 35 minutes.

Allow the pressure to reduce at room temperature. Take out pudding, remove the paper and serve.

To make the sauce (this can be done while the pressure is reducing), blend the egg yolks and sugar together in a bowl. Place the bowl over a pan of hot water on a low heat. Gradually add the apricot and lemon juices and whisk until the sauce is light, frothy and slightly thickened. Serve at once with the pudding.

PRE-STEAMING 15 minutes
COOKING TIME 35 minutes
PRESSURE low
SERVES 4–6

1 1-lb/450-g can apricot halves
3 oz/75 g castor sugar
3 oz/75 g butter
4 oz/100 g self-raising flour, sifted
4 tablespoons milk
2 egg whites
2 pints/generous 1 litre boiling water
Golden sauce
2 egg yolks
1 oz/25 g castor sugar
3 tablespoons apricot juice (from can)
1 teaspoon lemon juice

Traditional Chocolate Pudding

Cream the butter and sugar together until light and fluffy. Beat in the egg. Using a metal tablespoon, fold in the sieved flour and cocoa powder, together with the milk to give a soft mixture. Finally, fold in the sultanas.

Spoon the mixture into a well-greased 1½-pint (1-litre) pudding basin. Smooth the surface and cover with foil or a double layer of greased greaseproof paper tied securely under the rim.

Pour 2 pints (generous 1 litre) water into the cooker, place the trivet in the bottom and stand the pudding on the trivet. Pre-steam (see page 99) for 25 minutes, then bring to low pressure and cook for 25 minutes.

Allow the pressure to reduce at room temperature. Take out pudding, remove papers and turn onto a plate.

To make the sauce, break up the chocolate and put in a small bowl placed over a pan of hot water. When melted, stir in the butter and black coffee and serve.

PRE-STEAMING 25 minutes
COOKING TIME 25 minutes
PRESSURE low
SERVES 4–6

3 oz/75 g butter
3 oz/75 g castor sugar
1 large egg
3 oz/75 g self-raising flour
1 oz/25 g cocoa powder
1–2 tablespoons milk
1 oz/25 g sultanas
Mocha sauce
2 oz/50 g plain chocolate
2 oz/50 g butter
¼ pint/1.5 dl hot strong black coffee

Syrup Layer Pudding

PRE-STEAMING 15 minutes
COOKING TIME 30 minutes
PRESSURE low
SERVES 4

6 oz/175 g self-raising
 flour
¼ teaspoon salt
3 oz/75 g shredded suet
cold water to mix
4 tablespoons golden syrup
squeeze lemon juice
3–4 tablespoons fresh
 white breadcrumbs
2 pints/generous 1 litre
 boiling water

Sieve the flour and salt into a mixing bowl. Stir in the suet and mix in sufficient cold water to make a soft dough. Turn onto a floured board and roll out the pastry thinly. Cut into four rounds, one round large enough to fit into the bottom of a 1½-pint (1-litre) pudding basin, the other three each a little larger. Grease the basin thoroughly. Spread three rounds with golden syrup mixed with a little lemon juice and sprinkle with the breadcrumbs. Layer into the basin and top with the plain round leaving a 1-inch (2.5-cm) space at the top for the pudding to rise. Cover with foil or a double layer of greased greaseproof paper and secure under the rim with string.

Pour the water into the cooker and place the trivet in the bottom. Stand the pudding on the trivet. Pre-steam (see page 99) for 15 minutes. Bring to low pressure and cook for 30 minutes.

Allow the pressure to reduce at room temperature. Take out the pudding, remove the papers and turn onto a serving dish.

Lemon Dream

PRE-STEAMING 10 minutes
COOKING TIME 20 minutes
PRESSURE medium
SERVES 4–6

2 oz/50 g butter
2 oz/50 g castor sugar
3 eggs
3 oz/75 g self-raising
 flour
grated rind of 2 lemons
4 tablespoons lemon
 juice
11 tablespoons milk
2 pints/generous 1 litre
 boiling water
Decoration
flaked almonds, browned

This is a delicious pudding which when cooked has a lemon sauce at the bottom with a light sponge on top.

Cream the butter and sugar together until light and fluffy. Separate the eggs and beat the yolks into the creamed mixture, one at a time, adding a little of the sieved flour. Beat in the lemon rind and juice and stir in the milk. Fold in the remaining flour. Whisk the egg whites until stiff and, using a metal tablespoon, fold into the mixture.

Pour into a greased 2-pint (1.25-litre) pudding basin. Cover with foil or a double layer of greased grease-proof paper and secure under the rim with string.

Pour the boiling water into the cooker and place the trivet in the bottom. Stand the pudding on the trivet. Pre-steam (see page 99) for 10 minutes. Bring to medium pressure and cook for 20 minutes.

Allow the pressure to reduce at room temperature. Take out the pudding, remove the papers, and sprinkle the surface with a few browned flaked almonds. Serve.

Christmas Pudding with Brandy and Orange Butter

Make the puddings in advance of Christmas – about 6–8 weeks – so that they have time to mature. The brandy butter may be made about 4 weeks in advance and stored in the freezer or for 2 weeks in the refrigerator.

Providing your cooker is large enough, the puddings can be cooked simultaneously either side by side on the trivet, or if you have a high-dome cooker one on top of the other with the trivet in between, ensuring that there is sufficient space between the top basin and the vent so that if the pudding rises above the top of the basin it does not block the vent.

Sieve the flour, spice, nutmeg, cinnamon and salt into a mixing bowl. Stir in the breadcrumbs, sugar, suet, lemon rind and juice, currants, raisins, sultanas, peel and almonds. Mix in the treacle, eggs, brandy and sufficient milk or stout to give a firm consistency.

Divide the mixture between two well-greased 1-pint (0.75-litre) pudding basins. Cover with foil or a double layer of greased greaseproof paper and secure under the rim with string. Pour the water into the cooker and place the trivet in the bottom. Place the puddings on the trivet and pre-steam (see page 99) for 20 minutes. Bring to high pressure and cook for 1¾ hours.

Allow the pressure to reduce at room temperature. Take out the puddings and leave to cool. To store, replace the papers with new foil or a double layer of greaseproof paper and a piece of clean cloth firmly tied down. Store in a cool, airy place. During storage, more brandy may be added. Uncover, prick with a skewer and pour over 2–3 tablespoons brandy. Re-cover.

To reheat the puddings on Christmas Day, remove the cloth covering, pour 1 pint (6 dl) boiling water into the cooker and place the trivet in the bottom. Stand the puddings on the trivet, bring to high pressure and re-heat for 20 minutes. Allow the pressure to reduce at room temperature. Take off the covers and turn onto a serving dish. Pour over a little heated brandy and ignite.

To make the brandy butter, cream the butter and sugar together until fluffy. Gradually beat in the brandy to taste and the orange rind. Spoon into a serving dish, mark with a fork and spike the surface with almonds.

PRE-STEAMING 20 minutes
COOKING TIME 1¾ hours
RE-HEATING TIME 20 minutes
PRESSURE high
MAKES two 1-lb (450-g) puddings

2 oz/50 g plain flour
1 teaspoon mixed spice
½ teaspoon grated nutmeg
¼ teaspoon cinnamon
pinch salt
4 oz/100 g fresh white breadcrumbs
4 oz/100 g soft brown sugar
3 oz/75 g shredded suet
grated rind and juice of 1 lemon
2 oz/50 g currants
4 oz/100 g Valencia raisins
4 oz/100 g sultanas
4 oz/100 g mixed peel
2 oz/50 g blanched almonds, chopped
1 tablespoon black treacle
2 eggs, lightly beaten
1–2 tablespoons brandy
milk or stout to mix
2½ pints/1.25 litres boiling water
Brandy butter
6 oz/175 g unsalted butter
6 oz/175 g soft brown sugar
4–5 tablespoons brandy
finely grated rind of 1 orange
2 oz/50 g blanched almonds
Illustrated on page 112

Queen of Puddings

COOKING TIME 5 minutes
PRESSURE high
SERVES 4

½ pint/3 dl milk
1 oz/25 g butter
3 tablespoons fresh white
  breadcrumbs
1 tablespoon castor sugar
grated rind of 1 orange
2 egg yolks
½ pint/3 dl water
2 tablespoons thin-cut
  marmalade
Topping
2 egg whites
4 oz/100 g castor sugar

Place the milk and butter in a pan and heat to just below boiling. Remove from the heat and stir in the breadcrumbs, sugar and orange rind. Cover and leave to stand for 30 minutes. Mix well and stir in the egg yolks. Spoon the mixture into a greased ovenproof bowl or dish that can be accommodated in your cooker. Cover with foil or a double layer of greased greaseproof paper and tie under the rim.

Pour the water into the cooker, place the trivet in the bottom and put in the pudding. Bring to high pressure and cook for 5 minutes.

Allow the pressure to reduce at room temperature. Lift out the pudding and take off the paper. Carefully spread the marmalade over the surface.

To make the topping, whisk the egg whites until stiff. Fold in half the sugar and whisk until as stiff as before. With a metal tablespoon, fold in the remaining sugar. Spread the meringue over the marmalade and brown either under a pre-heated grill or at the top of a hot oven (450°F, 230°C, Gas Mark 8) for a few minutes. Serve at once.

Winter Fruit Compote

COOKING TIME 10 minutes,
  plus 10 minutes soaking
PRESSURE high
SERVES 4–6

6 oz/175 g prunes, stoned
4 oz/100 g figs
6 oz/175 g dried apricots
1 pint/6 dl boiling water
3 oz/75 g soft brown sugar
grated rind of 1 lemon
4 oz/100 g raisins
4 oz/100 g dates, chopped
Decoration
chopped nuts

Place the prunes, figs and apricots in a basin and pour over the boiling water. Cover with a plate and leave to soak for 10 minutes.

Place the fruits plus the soaking liquid in the cooker (with the trivet removed), making sure that the cooker is not more than half full. Add the sugar and lemon rind. Bring to high pressure and cook for 10 minutes.

Allow the pressure to reduce at room temperature. Stir in the raisins and dates. Allow to cool and serve sprinkled with chopped nuts; serve a bowl of whipped cream separately.

Crème Brûlée

This dish needs to be cooked a few hours before (or the day before) it is required so that the custard can be thoroughly chilled before the topping is added. It is a delicious dessert with a crunchy topping which contrasts with the creamy custard mixture.

Place the cream in a pan and bring almost to the boil. Pour onto the egg yolks and castor sugar, stirring well. Pour the mixture into a buttered soufflé or straight-sided ovenproof dish that can be accommodated in your cooker. Cover with foil or a double layer of greased greaseproof paper and secure under the rim.

Pour the water into the cooker, put the trivet in the bottom and stand the custard on the trivet. Bring to high pressure and cook for 5 minutes.

Allow the pressure to reduce at room temperature. Lift out the pudding and take off the papers. Allow to cool, then chill in the refrigerator.

About 30 minutes before serving, generously sprinkle the surface with a layer of soft brown sugar. Place under a pre-heated grill until the sugar begins to melt. Allow to cool before serving.

COOKING TIME 5 minutes
PRESSURE high
SERVES 4–6

1 pint/6 dl single cream
6 egg yolks
3 oz/75 g castor sugar
½ pint/3 dl water
Topping
soft brown sugar

Honeyed Pears

Peel the pears, but leave whole and do not remove the stalks.

Place the trivet in the base of the cooker and pour in the water. Stand the pears on the trivet and add the sugar, lemon rind and juice and honey. Bring to high pressure and cook for 4–8 minutes, depending on the hardness of the pears.

Allow the pressure to reduce at room temperature. Transfer the pears to a serving dish. Remove the trivet, return the open cooker to the heat and boil the cooking liquor until it becomes syrup. Spoon over the pears and chill. Serve with a bowl of whipped cream.

COOKING TIME 4–8 minutes
PRESSURE high
SERVES 4

4 cooking pears
½ pint/3 dl water
2 oz/50 g soft brown sugar
grated rind and juice of
  1 lemon
2–3 tablespoons clear
  honey
Illustrated opposite

Honeyed pears (see above)

Preserves

Marmalade, jams, jellies and chutneys can all be made in the pressure cooker with a great saving of time. The fruit for jam making (or peel for marmalade) is softened under pressure, but when the sugar has been added and dissolved the preserve is boiled in the open cooker until setting point is reached. With chutneys the ingredients are first softened under pressure, then boiled in the open cooker until the correct consistency is reached. The soft fruits (strawberries and raspberries) do not require this softening.

I still consider it an advantage to make your own marmalade and jams as the results are superior to the shop-bought varieties available. It also gives a tremendous sense of satisfaction to see the jars filled and neatly labelled.

Points to remember when making jams
1 Choose good quality fruit–not over-ripe or blemished. Certain fruits contain more natural pectin than others and will therefore set better. For fruits with a low pectin content it is necessary either to add lemon juice or mix the fruit with a proportion of a high pectin fruit. Low pectin fruits include strawberries, blackberries, cherries, pears, rhubarb and marrow. High pectin fruits include black and red currants, gooseberries and damsons.

Christmas pudding with brandy and orange butter (see page 108)

2 Sugar is added to preserves to enable them to have a long storage life. Preserving, lump or granulated sugar may be used. Preserving sugar is the most easily dissolved, but is not always available. It does help to warm the sugar in a low oven for about 5 minutes before adding it to the fruit.

3 Once the sugar has been added to the softened fruit and dissolved the preserve is boiled until the setting point is reached. This may take from 5–10 minutes, depending on the amount in the cooker and the size of the cooker, and also on how high the heat is. There are three ways to test a preserve for setting:

a The most accurate is the temperature test. When the sugar thermometer reaches 221°F (104°C) the preserve has reached setting point.

b Stir the preserve with a wooden spoon. Lift some of the preserve onto the spoon and hold it over the cooker for a few seconds. Allow the preserve to drop off the spoon–setting point has been reached when the preserve partly sets on the spoon.

c Spoon a little of the preserve onto a saucer. Leave to cool and then push your finger across the preserve. If the surface wrinkles, setting point has been reached.

When making marmalade in a pressure cooker, the peel is softened under pressure. When the sugar has been added the preserve is boiled in the open cooker.

Once setting point has been reached remove the cooker from the source of heat.

4 Skim the surface of the preserve with a draining spoon. Stir the preserve and ladle or pour from a measuring jug into clean, dry, warm jars. With a whole fruit jam, and marmalade, allow it to cool slightly in the cooker before potting to prevent the fruit rising to the tops of the jars. Allow to cool, then cover the surface with a waxed disc and finally a cellophane cover secured with a rubber band. Label each jar with the type of preserve and date it was made.

5 Store in a cool, dry place and use the preserves in rotation.

Making jam in the pressure cooker

1 Use medium pressure to soften the fruit for jam making; use high pressure to soften the peel for marmalade. The trivet is not used.

2 Do not fill the cooker more than half full with the prepared fruit and water for the softening process.

3 Allow the pressure to reduce at room temperature.

4 Use the cooker without the lid once the sugar has been added.

To adapt your own recipes for jams and marmalade for pressure cooking, reduce the liquid by half but ensure there is a minimum of $\frac{1}{2}$ pint (3 dl).

Lemon or Lime Marmalade

Wash the fruit and place in the cooker (with the trivet removed) with half the water, making sure that the cooker is not more than half full. Bring to high pressure and cook for 12 minutes.

Allow the pressure to reduce at room temperature. When cool enough to handle, take out the fruit and cut in halves. Remove the peel and cut into fine shreds. Place in the cooker with the water in which the fruit was softened. Scoop out the pips and pith and simmer in a pan with the remaining water for 10–15 minutes. Strain this liquid into the cooker. Add the warmed sugar and lemon juice and stir over a low heat until the sugar is completely dissolved. Increase the heat and boil in the open cooker until setting point is reached. Skim, cool slightly, then pot and label in the usual way.

COOKING TIME 12 minutes to soften fruit
PRESSURE high
MAKES about 5 lb (2.25 kg)

1½ lb/0.75 kg lemons or limes
1½ pints/9 dl water
3 lb/1.5 kg preserving, granulated or lump sugar
juice of 1 lemon

Three-Fruit Marmalade

Wash and dry the oranges, grapefruit and lemon. Halve and squeeze the juice from the lemon. Remove the coloured part of the peel from the oranges, grapefruit and lemon and cut into thin or thick strips according to whether you like a coarse-cut or thin-cut marmalade. (I find a potato peeler a good utensil to use for this operation as it is important not to include any pith with the peel.) Tie the pips and pith from the fruit in a muslin bag. Chop the flesh of the fruit coarsely.

Place the strips of peel and water in the cooker (with the trivet removed) making sure that the cooker is not more than half full. Add the muslin bag and leave to soak overnight.

The next day bring to high pressure and cook for 10–15 minutes, according to the thickness of the peel.

Allow the pressure to reduce at room temperature. Remove the lid and when cool enough to handle squeeze the muslin bag into the peel; discard the bag.

Return the open cooker to a low heat, add the warmed sugar, fruit pulp and lemon juice and stir until the sugar is totally dissolved. Increase the heat and boil

COOKING TIME 10–15 minutes to soften peel, plus overnight softening
PRESSURE high
MAKES about 5 lb (2.25 kg)

1½ lb/0.75 kg Seville oranges
1 grapefruit
1 lemon
1 pint/6 dl water
3 lb/1.5 kg preserving, granulated or lump sugar

rapidly in the open cooker until the setting point is reached.

Skim, cool slightly, then ladle or pour into warm jars. Cover with a waxed disc and when cold add a cellophane cover. Label and store.

Peach Jam

COOKING TIME 3 minutes
  to soften fruit
PRESSURE medium
MAKES about 3 lb (1.5 kg)

2 lb/1 kg peaches
½ pint/3 dl water
2 lb/1 kg preserving,
  granulated or lump sugar
juice of 1 lemon

Halve and stone the fruit. Place in the cooker (with the trivet removed) and add the water, making sure that the cooker is not more than half full. Bring to medium pressure and cook for 3 minutes.

Allow the pressure to reduce at room temperature. Remove the lid, add the warmed sugar and lemon juice. Return the open cooker to a low heat and stir until the sugar has completely dissolved. Increase the heat and boil in the open cooker until setting point is reached. Skim, cool slightly, then pot and label in the usual way.

Rhubarb and Orange Jam

COOKING TIME 5 minutes
  to soften peel
PRESSURE high
MAKES about 4 lb/1.75 kg

6 oranges
½ pint/3 dl water
juice of 2 lemons
3 lb/1.5 kg rhubarb, in
  2-inch (5-cm) lengths
3 lb/1.5 kg preserving,
  granulated or lump sugar

Wash and dry the oranges. Take off the peel and discard the white pith. Quarter the oranges, take out the pips and slice the flesh. Cut the orange peel into fine strips.

Place the peel and water in the cooker with the trivet removed, making sure that the cooker is not more than half full. Bring to high pressure and cook for 5 minutes.

Allow the pressure to reduce at room temperature. Remove the lid. Add the orange flesh, lemon juice, rhubarb and warmed sugar. Return the open cooker to a low heat and stir until the sugar has dissolved. Increase the heat and boil in the open cooker for about 10 minutes until setting point is reached. Skim, cool slightly, then pot and label in the usual way.

Jelly making

The same rules apply for jellies as given on page 113 for jam making. The most suitable fruits for jellies are blackcurrants, redcurrants, gooseberries and apples.

When making jellies it is essential that the fruit is completely softened and broken down in order for the acid and pectin contents to be released, therefore a pressure cooker is ideal for this process. When straining the cooked fruit, avoid the temptation to squeeze the bag as this will result in a cloudy-looking jelly. Reserve your smaller jars for potting jellies as they are best eaten as soon as possible after the jar has been opened.

With jellies it is difficult to give a yield as it depends on the amount of juice obtained from the fruit.

Apple Jelly

Wash the apples, discarding any bruised parts. Cut into thick slices without removing the peel, cores or pips. Place in the cooker (with the trivet removed) and add the lemon juice, cloves and water, making sure that the cooker is not more than half full. Bring to medium pressure and cook for 3 minutes.

Allow the pressure to reduce at room temperature. Remove the lid, mash the fruit, then strain it through a jelly bag or double thickness of a fine, clean cloth (a linen tea towel is ideal) suspended over a bowl.

Measure the strained juice and pour into the cooker with the trivet removed. Calculate the amount of sugar required and add to the cooker. Place over a low heat and stir until the sugar has completely dissolved. Increase the heat and boil rapidly in the open cooker until setting point is reached. Pour or ladle into small, warm jars. Cover the surfaces with a waxed circle. When cold, cover with a cellophane cover and secure with a rubber band. Label and store.

COOKING TIME 3 minutes
PRESSURE medium

3 lb/1.5 kg cooking apples
juice of 1 lemon
2–3 cloves (optional)
1 pint/6 dl water
1 lb/450 g preserving, granulated or lump sugar to each 1 pint/6 dl strained juice

Variations

Redcurrant jelly

Cook 3 lb (1.5 kg) redcurrants with ½ pint (3 dl) water at medium pressure for 1 minute. Strain and measure the juice. Allow 1¼ lb (600 g) sugar to each 1 pint (6 dl) strained juice. Continue as for apply jelly.

Blackcurrant jelly

Cook 3 lb (1.5 kg) blackcurrants with 1¾ pints (1 litre)

water at medium pressure for 5 minutes. Strain and measure the juice. Allow 1 lb (450 g) sugar to each 1 pint (6 dl) strained juice. Continue as for apple jelly.

Gooseberry jelly

Cook 3 lb (1.5 kg) gooseberries with 1 pint (6 dl) water at medium pressure for 5 minutes. Strain and measure the juice. Allow 1 lb (450 g) sugar to each 1 pint (6 dl) strained juice. Continue as for apply jelly.

Chutneys

When making pickles and chutney, the prepared vegetables are softened under high pressure. The chutney is then cooked in the open cooker until the correct consistency is reached.

Apart from the time factor, pressure cookers are ideal for making chutney because they are made from either stainless steel, aluminium, or coated with a non-stick surface. Pans and utensils which may give a metallic flavour to the chutney must not be used. Use nylon or hair sieves, stainless knives for chopping and a wooden spoon for stirring.

The flavour is better when chutney has matured. Store for 3–6 months before using, if you can!

Apricot Chutney (Hot)

COOKING TIME 20 minutes, plus 1 hour soaking
PRESSURE high
MAKES about 4 lb (1.75 kg)

8 oz/225 g dried apricots
1 lb/450 g raisins
1 lb/0.5 kg onions
1¼ pints/7.5 dl vinegar
1 tablespoon salt
2 teaspoons cayenne pepper
2 oz/50 g ground ginger
1 oz/25 g coriander seeds
1 lb/450 g sugar
2 tablespoons made mustard

This chutney makes an excellent side dish to a curry.

Place the apricots in a bowl and cover with boiling water. Leave to soak for 1 hour.

Chop the raisins, onions and drained apricots. Place the prepared onions in the cooker (with the trivet removed), pour in the vinegar and simmer in the open cooker for 10 minutes. Add the apricots, raisins, salt, cayenne pepper, ginger, and coriander seeds tied in a muslin bag, making sure that the cooker is not more than half full. Bring to high pressure and cook for 20 minutes.

Allow the pressure to reduce at room temperature. Remove the lid, take out the muslin bag and stir well. Stir in the sugar and mustard. Return to a low heat to dissolve the sugar, then boil the chutney in the open cooker for about 10 minutes, until it has a thick consistency. (Remember to stir the chutney occasionally.)

Check the seasoning and ladle into hot jars. Cover, label and store.

Apple and Date Chutney

Peel, core and dice the apples. Chop the onions and dates. Place the apples, onions, dates, sultanas and half the vinegar in the cooker (with the trivet removed), making sure that the cooker is not more than half full. Bring to medium pressure and cook for 12 minutes.

Allow the pressure to reduce at room temperature. Remove the lid, stir in the remaining vinegar, the sugar, salt, ginger, mustard and cayenne pepper. Return the open cooker to a low heat and stir until the sugar has dissolved. Continue cooking in the open cooker until the mixture becomes thick, stirring frequently. Check the seasoning, then ladle into warm jars. Cover, label and store.

COOKING TIME 12 minutes
PRESSURE medium
MAKES about 4½ lb (2 kg)

2 lb/1 kg cooking apples
1 lb/0.5 kg onions
1 lb/450 g dates
4 oz/100 g sultanas
½ pint/3 dl malt vinegar
8 oz/225 g soft brown
  sugar
1 teaspoon salt
1 teaspoon ground ginger
pinch dry mustard
pinch cayenne pepper

Green Tomato Chutney

Slice the tomatoes thinly. Peel, core and chop the apples. Place the tomatoes, apples, onions, raisins, garlic, salt, cayenne pepper, ginger and half the vinegar in the cooker (with the trivet removed), making sure that the cooker is not more than half full. Bring to high pressure and cook for 10 minutes.

Reduce the pressure with cold water. Remove the lid, stir in the sugar and remaining vinegar. Return the open cooker to the heat and simmer until the chutney thickens, stirring from time to time. Ladle into warm jars. Cover, label and store.

COOKING TIME 10 minutes
PRESSURE high
MAKES about 3 lb (1.5 kg)

2 lb/1 kg green tomatoes
2 cooking apples
2 onions or 8 oz/225 g
  shallots, chopped
6 oz/175 g raisins or
  sultanas
1 clove garlic, crushed
½ teaspoon salt
½ teaspoon cayenne pepper
¼ teaspoon ground ginger
¾ pint/4.5 dl malt vinegar
6 oz/175 g soft brown
  sugar

Bottling

Both fruit and vegetables may be preserved by bottling. To a certain extent I feel that the advent of the freezer has superseded this method of preservation. However, with the aid of the pressure cooker, and for non-freezer owners, bottling may be carried out quickly and safely. It is certainly preferable to preserve a glut of fruit which would otherwise go to waste or you would become thoroughly bored with. I do not consider it worthwhile bottling vegetables as a variety of fresh vegetables is obtainable all the year round, and a wide selection of frozen vegetables is available from your local store or supermarket.

Method for bottling fruit
1 Wash and rinse the jars and lids well—use kilner-type jars, or the clip-top type. Stand them in boiling water until ready to use.
2 Prepare the fruit, according to kind. Fruit for bottling should be firm, ripe and undamaged. For best results, ensure that the fruit put into each jar is of even size. When preparing fruits which discolour after peeling put them into lightly salted water and before packing into the jars rinse in cold water.
3 Pack the fruit firmly into the jars, filling each jar to the shoulder.
4 Pour in the boiling syrup leaving a $\frac{1}{4}$-inch (5-mm) space at the top as the fruit will make some of its own juice. When pouring in the syrup, do this a little at a time and release the air bubbles by tapping the base of the jar on a board. Choose a syrup suitable for the eventual use of the fruit. For example, a light syrup is better for fruits intended for pies and tarts, and other cooked dishes. If you intend to serve the fruit on its own, use a heavy syrup.

To make the syrup, place the sugar and water in a pan. Dissolve over a low heat, then bring to the boil and boil for 1 minute.

Light syrup 1 pint (6 dl) water to 2–4 oz (50–100 g) granulated or lump sugar.

Heavy syrup 1 pint (6 dl) water to 6–8 oz (175–225 g) granulated or lump sugar.

5 Fit the tops to the jars. Screw metal bands down until tight, then unscrew a quarter of a turn. If using clips to secure the lids there is sufficient give to allow for the escape of air and steam during processing. Stand the filled jars in hot water.

6 Place the trivet in the base of the cooker and pour in 2 pints (1.25 litres) boiling water. Using a pair of oven gloves, lift the jars onto the trivet making sure that they do not touch each other or the sides of the cooker.

7 Place the cooker on a moderate heat, bring to low pressure and cook for time given in the chart below.

8 Allow the pressure to reduce at room temperature.

9 Using oven gloves, lift out the jars and tighten the screw lids. (Those jars with clips will seal themselves during pressure cooking.)

10 The following day, test the seal of the jars by un-screwing the bands or removing the clips. Lift each jar by the cover–it should not move. Replace band, dried and greased to prevent rusting. Label the jars and store in a cool and preferably dark place.

You may like to bottle different fruits together in the same jars–for example blackberries and apples. Any fruits may be put together providing they have the same cooking time. If using fruits which require varying times, calculate the time according to the fruit which requires the longest processing time.

When bottling fruit in a pressure cooker, it is important to choose firm, ripe and undamaged fruit.

Fruit	Preparation	Cooking time at low pressure
Apples	Peel and core. Cut into quarters or slices and drop into lightly salted water. Rinse before packing into the jars.	1 minute
Apricots	Halve and remove stones or leave whole. If bottling whole, prick with a fork.	1 minute
Blackberries	Pick over and discard any stalks and over-ripe fruit. Wash and drain.	1 minute
Blackcurrants and redcurrants	Strip from the stalks. Wash and drain.	1 minute
Cherries	Remove stalks. Halve and stone or process whole.	1 minute
Damsons, greengages and plums	Leave whole and prick with a fork or halve and stone.	1 minute
Gooseberries	Choose hard, green gooseberries, otherwise they will burst during processing.	1 minute
Peaches	Remove skins, halve and stone. (Slice if large.)	Halves 3 minutes Slices 1 minute
Pears	Peel and core. Drop into lightly salted water. Rinse before packing into jars.	3 minutes
Raspberries	Pick over and discard stalks and over-ripe fruit.	1 minute
Rhubarb	Discard leaves and stalk ends. Cut into even-sized lengths. Pack tightly.	Forced rhubarb 1 minute Garden rhubarb 2 minutes
Strawberries	Pick over and discard stalks and over-ripe fruit.	3 minutes

Sauces

The recipes in this chapter, although not all cooked in a pressure cooker, have a place in this book as, for example, many fish and vegetable dishes are enhanced by the addition of a suitable sauce. Sauces are not difficult to make and may be prepared while the food is cooking in the pressure cooker. Most sauces freeze well, so you may find it an advantage to prepare more than you need and freeze the remainder. Freeze sauces in foil bags or polythene containers, leaving a small headspace. Egg-based sauces such as mayonnaise and hollandaise do not freeze successfully.

Tomato Sauce

Heat the butter in the open cooker (with the trivet removed) and sauté the bacon, onion and carrot for 2–3 minutes. Add the tomatoes, bay leaf, tomato purée, Worcestershire sauce, basil, seasoning, sugar and stock, making sure that the cooker is not more than half full. Bring to high pressure and cook for 5 minutes.

Allow the pressure to reduce at room temperature. Remove the bay leaf. Sieve, or blend the slightly cooled sauce in the liquidiser. Check and adjust the seasoning as necessary.

COOKING TIME 5 minutes
PRESSURE high
MAKES 1 pint (6 dl)

½ oz/15 g butter
1–2 rashers streaky bacon, chopped
1 onion, chopped
1 carrot, sliced
1 14-oz/397-g can tomatoes
1 bay leaf
2 teaspoons tomato purée
few drops Worcestershire sauce
½ teaspoon basil
salt and pepper
pinch sugar
½ pint/3 dl stock or water

Béchamel Sauce

MAKES ½ pint (3 dl)

½ pint/3 dl milk
1 carrot
1 onion
1 bay leaf
3–4 peppercorns
1 oz/25 g butter
1 oz/25 g plain flour
salt and pepper

Place the milk in a pan. Add the whole carrot and onion, the bay leaf and peppercorns. Place over a low heat and bring to the boil. Remove from the heat and allow to infuse for 15 minutes.

Melt the butter in a pan. Remove from the heat and stir in the flour. Return to the heat and cook for 1–2 minutes, stirring. Remove from the heat and gradually stir in the strained milk. Return to the heat and, stirring, bring to the boil. Cook for 2–3 minutes. Season and serve.

Variations

Caper sauce Stir 2 tablespoons drained capers into the sauce.

Cheese sauce Stir 2 oz (50 g) grated cheese and a pinch of dry mustard into the sauce. Once the cheese has been added do not allow the sauce to boil.

Egg sauce Stir 1 finely chopped hard-boiled egg into the sauce.

Mushroom sauce Stir 2 oz (50 g) chopped mushrooms, sautéed in a little butter, into the sauce.

Onion sauce Stir 2 boiled, chopped onions into the sauce.

Parsley sauce Stir 2–3 tablespoons finely chopped parsley into the sauce.

Anchovy sauce Stir a few drops anchovy essence into the sauce.

Mayonnaise

MAKES ½ pint (3 dl)

2 egg yolks
salt and pepper
¼ teaspoon dry mustard
½ pint/3 dl oil
2 tablespoons wine vinegar

Place the egg yolks and seasonings in a bowl and lightly whisk to combine the ingredients. Whisking all the time, add the oil *drop by drop* until the mixture thickens. Stir in the vinegar which will thin the mayonnaise. Check the seasoning and adjust if necessary.

Store in an airtight container in the refrigerator.

Variation

Tartare sauce Stir 2–3 teaspoons each chopped chives, capers, gherkins and parsley into the mayonnaise.

Hollandaise Sauce

Boil the vinegar, peppercorns and water in a pan until reduced by one third, then strain into a bowl placed over a pan of hot water. Add the egg yolks and cook over the heat until the mixture thickens, stirring. Add the butter, piece by piece, and beat or whisk into the sauce. Season to taste and add a few drops of lemon juice. Serve at once.

MAKES ½ pint (3 dl)

2 tablespoons wine vinegar
4 peppercorns
4 tablespoons water
3 egg yolks
6 oz/175 g butter
salt and pepper
few drops lemon juice

Variation
Mousseline sauce Stir 2–3 tablespoons lightly whipped cream into hollandaise sauce just before serving. Serve with salmon, vegetable and chicken dishes.

Bolognaise Sauce

Heat the butter in the open cooker (with the trivet removed) and sauté the bacon, onion, carrots, celery and garlic for 2–3 minutes. Stir in the minced beef and cook for a further 2–3 minutes, until browned. Add the stock, red wine, tomatoes, seasoning, mushrooms and pepper, making sure that the cooker is not more than half full. Bring to high pressure and cook for 15 minutes.

Allow the pressure to reduce at room temperature. Return the open cooker to the heat and cook the sauce for 2–3 minutes, to allow it to reduce and thicken. Check the seasoning and serve with pasta, tossed in melted butter and grated nutmeg.

COOKING TIME 15 minutes
PRESSURE high
MAKES 1½ pints (9 dl)

1 oz/25 g butter
2 rashers streaky bacon, chopped
1 onion, chopped
2 carrots, sliced
1 stick celery, chopped
1 clove garlic, crushed
1 lb/0.5 kg minced beef
½ pint/3 dl stock
¼ pint/1.5 dl red wine
1 10-oz/275-g can tomatoes
salt and pepper
4 oz/100 g mushrooms, sliced
1 green pepper, seeded and chopped

Index